Join our interactive online community
at www.UnfairAdvantageBooks.com

Published by CelebrityPress™, Orlando, FL
A division of The Celebrity Branding Agency®

Celebrity Branding® is a registered trademark
Printed in the United States of America.

ISBN: 978-0-9853643-8-0
LCCN: 2012939933

This publication is designed to provide accurate and authoritative information with regard to the subject matter covered. It is sold with the understanding that the publisher is not engaged in rendering legal, accounting, or other professional advice. If legal advice or other expert assistance is required, the services of a competent professional should be sought. The opinions expressed by the authors in this book are not endorsed by CelebrityPress™ and are the sole responsibility of the author rendering the opinion.

Most CelebrityPress™ titles are available at special quantity discounts for bulk purchases for sales promotions, premiums, fundraising, and educational use. Special versions or book excerpts can also be created to fit specific needs.

For more information, please write:

CelebrityPress™
520 N. Orlando Ave, #2
Winter Park, FL 32789

or call 1.877.261.4930

Visit us online at www.CelebrityPressPublishing.com

UNFAIR
ADVANTAGE

Contents

SOLVING THE PUZZLE

INTRODUCTION

The Fear Stops Here

By Brian Pasch

As I travel across the country speaking with automotive professionals, there's a consensus that the pace of change in our industry is akin to being strapped to a rocket ship. It's not uncommon to hear dealers and managers confess: "I know I'm missing some opportunities, but I only know what I know!"

Automotive executives must keep pace with ever-changing state, federal and franchise mandates; that alone can be a full-time job! Today, they also must have strategic conversations for their businesses on social media, search engine optimization, pay-per-click advertising, retargeting, mobile marketing, chat, website merchandising, market pricing tools, online video marketing, and dealership mobile apps.

Where their jobs often get frustrating is when they attempt to integrate these opportunities with traditional media channels in an effort to operate their businesses effectively and profitably. One dealer principal confiding in me said:

> "Brian, I stopped taking calls from people like you. *(His comment took me back a second. I needed to figure out just "who" I was!)* I have a hard time understanding digital marketing peddlers, and I don't like to sound stupid. *(He thought I was a peddler. Good, I could work with that.)* Heck, I don't even know how to inspect your digital marketing ideas to know if they work. I'll just keep doing what I've been doing in the past because I'm comfortable with those choices. I know that I'll miss some good ideas, but that's my choice."

Needless to say, I was able to educate and demonstrate why this dealer needed to change with the times. I built a bridge of understanding that "connected the dots" from the successful strategies he developed before the internet to today's marketing opportunities. In the end, he thanked me for not allowing him to sabotage his business based on personal bias and fear.

Are you feeling a little uncomfortable with the pace of change in automotive retailing? More than a little? How about overwhelmed? Wherever your comfort level is today, this book was designed to meet the needs of automotive professionals who want an Unfair Advantage.

When Tracy and I first discussed writing a book together, one thought was to create a handbook covering the latest winning strategies in automotive marketing and branding. However, as we surveyed the needs of dealers, it was clear that the scope of our book should be expanded. For example, one of the biggest profit leaks in dealerships today is how phone calls and internet leads are handled. Dealers were asking for suggestions on scripts, processes and workflows.

We also found that few dealers were embracing mobile technology, despite that fact that 20 percent of website traffic in 2012 is coming from mobile and tablet devices. Mobile websites, mobile inspection tools, and custom-branded mobile apps give dealers new ways to connect with consumers who choose to conduct research and primarily communicate using their smartphones.

In every area of dealership operations we noted that change was in the air of boardroom meetings and on showroom floors. The challenge was to carefully reflect on those dealership conversations to see how Tracy and I could resolve their needs.

Based on dealer feedback, our new vision was to create a list of "hot topics" and create a new operating handbook for automotive professionals. Once we reviewed the list, it was clear that in order to create an authoritative guide we would need contributing authors to pen chapters from their area of expertise.

Tracy and I were blessed by the responses we received from industry leaders and subject matter experts. The authors were in agreement that dealers needed an updated reference for automotive operations, training, marketing and branding.

Each chapter is focused on winning solutions and/or strategies that are working at leading dealerships. Together these chapters represent a checklist of powerful ideas that readers can use to inspect their dealership's current strategies, processes and operations.

For some readers, this book represents a massive change in dealership thinking and operations. If this applies to you, don't allow yourself to be discouraged. Make a checklist of the actions needed and prioritize them based on the anticipated benefit to the dealership.

Take one step at a time. Readers cannot afford to ignore the changes that are happening in the automotive industry. Dealers that fail to fully embrace the new consumer marketing and communication paradigms will continue to lose market share.

For others, there will be strategies covered in the chapters that are already in place. If so, congratulations for keeping up with the pace of change. Even progressive dealers will find many new ideas in this book that can be implemented to increase their market share and cripple their competition.

Unfair Advantage is designed to provide actionable ideas for all areas of dealership responsibility. This book is for dealer principals, general managers, general sales managers, sales professionals, fixed operations directors, internet sales managers, social media specialists, and anyone who wants to be a leader in the automotive industry.

Recognizing how change impacts printed books, you'll be pleased to know that updates to the strategies introduced in this book will be published in an online website community created by the authors and joined by passionate automotive professionals. Visit www.UnfairAdvantageBooks.com to register and engage with other dealers who want an edge—an *Unfair Advantage*!

Let's get our journey started.

—*Brian Pasch*

WELCOME TO THE NEIGHBORHOOD!

These days, it seems like you have to be an expert on virtually everything to succeed as a car dealer. One minute you are worrying about having the best website, next you are trying to figure out how to get it found in search engines, then you are focused on the follow-up systems within the dealership. Some of these areas are so new and so fast moving that you can't be on top of all of them and still run your business successfully. Yet, at the same time, you can't afford to neglect any of them if you want to succeed in today's marketplace. Then, on top of all that, you have to find time to stay at the cutting edge of the area your customers expect you to know all about—cars!

I often think of running my auto dealership as being a bit like doing a jigsaw puzzle. You have all these pieces you have to fit together to create the outcome you want and then you discover that just one missing piece can mean the whole thing ends in disappointment.

However, the truth is that running a dealership is a lot more difficult than doing a jigsaw puzzle. At least with a jigsaw puzzle, you start out with all the right pieces and with a picture on the front of the box to guide you. In running your dealership, you have to decide what you want the picture on the box to be—what kind of dealership you want to build and how you want to work. You then have to work out what pieces you need before you can even start putting them together. And here's what makes it most challenging—the pieces you need to put into place are changing all the time as so many areas are moving so fast. In areas like the internet and social media, a month is a long time, and you can so easily fall behind if you don't have the right help and advice.

MEETING THE CHALLENGE

It was the combination of all those challenges that motivated Brian and I to create this book. It's also what made us realize that we needed to create something different from the usual collection of tips and advice. We wanted to create something to give you the most important pieces you must put in place to complete your puzzle. And we wanted to make sure the advice remained relevant, up-to-date and easy to apply.

We realized that nobody could even pretend to be an expert on all of the areas we wanted to cover. We figured it was far more important for you to be able to find the right expertise quickly. So we decided to put together a top team of specialists who could provide cutting-edge insight in each of the areas that matter most. We are honored to have assembled a group of top experts who have applied their knowledge to the specific needs of people in the auto business.

We wanted something that would give auto dealers like you easy access to a good overview of the main issues you need to be on top of if you want to build your business. It also had to allow you to drill down into greater detail in whatever area is most important for your needs right now.

However, we felt that just giving you access to lots of information was not enough, no matter how good the information. The fact is too many books like this get out of date quickly and become less relevant. We wanted a resource that was the opposite. We wanted this to stay up-to-date in a fast-changing world, and we wanted it to grow in relevance over time. That's why we decided to add a crucial additional benefit.

CREATING A COMMUNITY

As part of this book, we have created a powerful online community where each of the experts featured here will provide updates and enhancements to the strategies and insights they share. This will ensure that the content remains relevant and at the leading edge as technology changes and experience gets updated. But more than that, this community will extend beyond updates from the featured authors.

As part of the community, you will get the chance to add your thoughts, questions and insights. At the same time, the community will be enhanced by the contributions of other professionals with practical experience at the cutting edge of running auto dealerships.

That way, this book will become a living guide to the strategies you need to master to build the success of your dealership. In a way, it will help you keep the picture on the front of the jigsaw puzzle box up-to-date; it will help you identify the pieces you need, and it will show you where to go first. It is your guide on how to put the pieces together faster and more efficiently than you ever could without this expertise at your fingertips.

So let's look a bit more at what is covered within these pages. We have identified five different segments that provide the most important pieces you need to put in place to complete your jigsaw.

1. Foundations

2. Technology

3. Process

4. Operations

5. Marketing

FOUNDATIONS

A successful dealership needs strong basics, so we start out by explaining how you can position your dealership in the best way possible. You need to be seen as the go-to dealer in your area and establish your own expertise in the minds of your target market.

You then need to be able to communicate your expertise easily in all channels. That's not just about following up the latest social media ideas. You need to be able to control all the engagement with your customers and prospects to keep your message consistent and make sure it is delivered effectively.

TECHNOLOGY

While technology is opening up huge opportunities for those who know how to take advantage of it, it can be intimidating for people who don't want to see themselves as geeks—or who don't have a friendly teenager handy who can advise them.

Most of us don't know if that latest website idea will transform our dealership into the market leader or will be a total waste of time and money that will need to be replaced a few months later. But it's not only hard to know the difference; it's often difficult to know whose advice we can trust. That's why we assembled expert guides not only to highlight what technology you need to focus on in your dealership but also to point out the key actions you need to take to get the best results possible.

PROCESS

Despite the growing dominance of technology and online channels, the most successful businesses also master the traditional forms of communication such as face-to-face selling and telephone techniques. So, in looking at process, we've covered what you really should know about areas such as sales training and telephone skills to make sure they are integrated with your technology and internet use.

OPERATIONS

No matter how successful you are in all the other aspects, it's vital to get the operations part of your dealership right if you want to succeed. We'll talk about topics such as pricing, merchandising and reinsurance. While these topics may seem less exciting than the latest social media gimmick, it's getting these parts right that makes customers actually buy from you—and keep coming back.

MARKETING

Getting your marketing right can help you attract a steady stream of new customers to help you grow your business. But, depending on the approach you choose, you can either spend huge amounts of money for very little return, or you can get steady streams of profitable new customers for not much outlay.

The right advice here can make a huge difference to your bottom line. For example, knowing how to optimize your website for search engines or harness the power of video marketing can help you quickly and easily become the dominant choice in your area for very little outlay.

You really need a whole team of experts to address the most important issues in this area. That's what we've aimed to create in this book.

MORE THAN INFORMATION

But we wanted to make sure that this wasn't just a whole lot of information. You should be able to identify what's most important and start applying it right away. A valuable part of this process is therefore the real-life case studies we've included. These show how others have approached these issues and succeeded with them. We'll also show you what you need to do to turn this information into the best possible plan of action for your dealership.

Overall, what we've aimed to do in this book is help you get a clear picture of what you need to do to make your dealership more successful and profitable in the current economy.

Going back to my jigsaw puzzle analogy, we're going to help you be very clear about your aims—the picture on the front of your box. We'll then make sure you know what pieces you need to put in place and help you identify the best way to put them together for your specific needs.

And, because these days the puzzle keeps changing, the information and guidance you get will be continually updated through the living community you have joined.

Welcome to our community!

—Tracy Myers

CHAPTER 1

Supercharged Vehicle Merchandising

By George Nenni

Vehicle merchandising is one of my favorite subjects, having worked for many years at Dealer Specialties, the merchandising pioneer for new and used vehicles. In the automotive industry, vehicle merchandising is the acquisition, preparation, organization, and presentation of vehicles both on a dealer's physical lot and online. Vehicle merchandising allows dealers to market the right cars in the most professional, consistent and attractive manner possible to shoppers.

Consumers are making a high-dollar investment when they purchase a car. They need to be sure the dealership and the car they found in inventory are the right choices. Putting in the time and effort into vehicle merchandising maximizes the dealership's opportunity to engage the car shopper and win them over to their store.

Before the internet, vehicle merchandising focused on the presentation of inventory on the physical dealership lot. When the automotive dot-com boom began, it was nearly impossible to convince dealers that placing a single 320-x-240-pixel digital photo online would drive sales. Today, 16-plus photos, along with videos, vehicle history, inspection data and dealer comments, are standard operating procedure.

In this chapter, I will share specific strategies to improve merchandising through photography, video and vehicle descriptions. These strategies will increase leads per vehicle, drive engagement for specific vehicles, and increase post-sale satisfaction for buyers.

PHOTOGRAPHY

Digital Hardware Quality

No merchandising conversation is complete without discussing proper tools. In the case of photography, success depends on the quality and variety of digital photos captured. When purchasing a digital camera, you get what you pay for; most of the investment goes toward the quality of the lens.

The camera lens attempts to duplicate the human eye. The lens sees a vehicle, focuses, and then transmits color, sharpness and brightness to the digital storage device. Expensive lenses have higher-quality glass with the lowest levels of distortion, making the picture "pop."

For vehicle photos, the best setup is a wide-angle lens attached to a digital SLR camera. This allows dealers to capture as much width as needed at a reasonable distance. Polarizing lenses are great for outdoor shots of cars, since they remove sun glare and dramatically improve the quality of photos.

The digital SLR camera also provides control of the f-stop (the aperture) and exposure (how fast the aperture opens and closes). This allows the camera to make the most of the natural light provided. Since the subject matter (the vehicle) is not moving, take advantage of this by reducing the size of your aperture, increasing the photo sharpness. Place the camera on a tripod to keep it perfectly still, which will allow for exceptionally sharp photos.

Angles and Number of Photos

Sixteen photos per car is average, however, some dealers approach 100 photos per car. When selling remotely, where the buyer will not inspect the vehicle before purchasing, take more than 24 photos per vehicle. Today's consumers expect a full virtual experience when shopping online.

Dealers can determine the number of photos by asking the question, "What do I want to capture?" Be intentional when placing vehicle photos online. Start with a simple plan to make sure all the basics are covered, including:

- **Exterior:** All cars have four sides and four corners, so capturing those eight shots makes sense. Zoom in on at least one wheel.

- **Interior:** One shot of each opened door and trunk is a good practice, since consumers want to see the quality of each seat and surrounding areas. You can also capture nice front-seat shots from the back seat. For third-row vehicles, capture one or two pictures showing the row disappearing into the floor, or being removed.

- **Options:** Show them off. An image of a sunroof makes a good value-building picture.

- **Technology Advancements:** Unique characteristics: technology advancements, leather interior, heated seats, premium wheels and tires, wood-grain dash, etc., should be highlighted with additional photos.

- **Defects:** Dealers have embraced a more transparent approach to selling used vehicles. If there are defects in the vehicle that you are unable, or unwilling to remedy, then consider disclosing this information. The buyer will eventually learn of these issues and will trust you more if you are upfront in the beginning.

- **Thumbnail Photo:** The first shot is typically the "thumbnail" shot, shown on search-results pages. Since people read left-to-right, the first shot should be the driver's-side front corner. This way, all vehicles will point in the same direction; organized, sharp and uniform.

VEHICLE VIDEOS

How should a dealer's approach to videos differ from that of photos? Consider the differences. Videos offer motion and sound. If customers want to see a vehicle's quality, there is no better way than by taking high-quality still photos. Videos allow voice-over and motion, as well as real-life branding for the dealership.

When it comes to the quality of the video camera, you don't need to break the bank. A camera-phone or an inexpensive HD video camera will do nicely. Look for video camera models that also have an audio input jack for a microphone. This allows you to use a wireless microphone to eliminate background or ambient noise.

There are two primary types of vehicle videos: 1) pan and scan (P&S), where still images are stitched together and made to look like a video, or 2) real video.

P&S videos are cost-effective. The P&S video includes background music with a voice-over of the featured vehicle as well as introduction and closing footage. These videos normally begin and end with dealer-branded information, with vehicle-specific content in between.

Dealers do not need a professional production company to create real vehicle videos. They do, however, need a plan. If the video includes a walk-around, dealers must decide which features to highlight. Will they pop the hood, fold down the third row, turn on the stereo, and start the vehicle?

In the same way that photos are specific to each vehicle, the video script should be treated the same way. Have someone knowledgeable discuss the vehicle in a pleasant, clear voice. Discuss the features and options that make the vehicle attractive. Include in the script special options, mileage, number of owners, third-party awards, or even the estimated MPG.

UNIQUE VEHICLE DESCRIPTIONS

With photos and videos completed, dealers must dive into the vehicle's text description if they want to maximize the potential of their vehicle detail page (VDP). Not as concerned with vehicle descriptions? Your competitors are. Savvy dealers offer rich vehicle descriptions, by including marketing comments and relevant options. Remember to stay away from all caps, since it gives the impression you are shouting and is also difficult to read.

Begin descriptions with VIN decoding. There are severe limits to VIN decoded information, so use this as a starting point. The VIN can only definitively confirm the year, make, model, body style, engine and some safety options. Half the time, the VIN recognizes trim levels, though results vary by OEM.

Software with algorithms comparing the VIN to other known information can determine trim level, options, fuel-efficiency and more. If dealers are able to access OEM codes from their DMS, they can be decoded for new vehicle inventory. Remember, not all VIN decoding and reverse-configuration programs are the same, so have several vendors decode these for accuracy.

Ideally, dealers should try to purchase both inventory management tools and websites from common vendors, or at the very least vendors that have standardized the data descriptions. In order to optimize the consumer shopping experience, vehicle data must be collected, decoded and described in the same way a dealer's website searches for it. Data within the website search categories, such as trim level or GPS availability, must be "normalized" so the website is able to locate and present the features appropriately.

For example, vehicle colors present data conflicts. How many different ways can an OEM describe the color "white"? Pearl white, metallic white, or arctic white are ways "white" cars come labeled from the factory. Every OEM has unique descriptions, but the consumer doesn't know that. If a consumer is looking for a "white" vehicle, they use the search term "white." Dealers should put their vendors to the test, making sure vehicle details allow flexible and granular searches.

What else should be included in the vehicle description? Is the vehicle certified, either by the OEM or a third party? Does the vehicle include a history report from CARFAX or other reputable providers? Does the vehicle inspection contain data on paint thickness, tire depth, etc.? After all, the unique features provide better gross profit on each vehicle. Once the consumer realizes that is the "must-have" vehicle, the price paid can provide the dealership with the desired margin.

Let's not forget marketing descriptions, which are the "online salesperson" discussing vehicles in a conversational way and creating a sense of urgency. If not written by someone on staff, evaluate the various software systems that write customized marketing descriptions. Consumers don't want to just know the features of the vehicle; they want to be sold. Text marketing descriptions should convince consumers that the car is perfect for them!

Price

One of the most important pieces of text in any vehicle description is the price. Dealer opinion has truly evolved on providing price. During the early days of the internet, with only 200,000 units online, popular opinion was "I want to make them call me to get a price!"

Today, with millions of vehicles online, consumers use the internet to educate themselves. Shoppers skip over cars lacking prices. Since vehicles are displayed on automotive portals, such as GetAuto.com, Cars.com, and AutoTrader.com, prices must be competitive.

In order for shoppers to seriously consider vehicles, they must be priced within an acceptable range. There are software tools on the market that can ensure dealers price competitively. If a vehicle needs to be priced higher than what the software recommends, practicing the merchandising techniques outlined in this chapter will help drive success.

Since merchandising is about shelf-space, it's important to showcase vehicle listings and images in front of the right buyers at the right time. This inventory distribution process is called syndication. Proper syndication should increase calls, leads and walk-in traffic to the dealership.

With choices including automotive portals, local online classified sites and dealer websites, determining a strategy of where to send vehicle listings can be confusing to the dealer. Which syndication platform delivers the best ROI?

Websites such as eBay and Craigslist require special tactics but can deliver a very high ROI. Dealers must experiment with their syndication partners. Use conversion data, analytics, ad success rates and online metrics to evaluate syndication partners.

When dealers review their syndication strategy, questions will arise:

- How much do SRPs, VDPs and leads cost?
- Can I track consumer behavior with multi-channel sales funnels?
- How much should I budget to sell a vehicle?
- What are the closing rates on these leads?

Dealers should consider integrating a CRM system to facilitate these answers. With CRM software, dealers can track data starting from the shopping process through the buying process. Advanced CRM software will also show the keywords, referring sites or paid search investments that generated a lead.

The next question for effective inventory syndication is, "What is the optimal execution strategy?" The two most important things to keep in mind are:

1. Have one database with accurate information feeding your syndication, and

2. Syndication should be as close to real-time as possible.

Why is a single database handling syndication? Without it, control and consistency are lost. Multiple databases mean multiple updates for each vehicle that is changed. Multiple databases increase the potential for erroneous information.

Dealers must update inventory online as fast as possible, including any price changes. The faster dealers turn their inventory, the sooner their investment is recovered. How many times does a dealer sell a car for more money than listed online? Sold vehicles should be removed instantly, not after 24 hours.

ON-THE-LOT MERCHANDISING IS STILL IMPORTANT

In many ways the internet has made shopping more efficient, allowing consumers to determine a shortlist of interesting vehicles. Consumers still visit dealerships, take test drives, and leave in new vehicles.

On-the-lot vehicle merchandising starts with good-looking facilities, and clean, organized vehicles with relevant information easily at hand. Regardless of which vehicle brings them to the lot, consumers arrive curious and will check out other vehicles. Inventory should have professional, on-the-vehicle merchandising elements, starting with window stickers.

Since new cars come with stickers from the factory, dealers should use full-color window labels for their used vehicles. Window stickers should include dealer logos, branding, and connections to current advertising campaigns.

Information on the stickers should be clean, clear and easy to read. There is virtually no limit to the amount of information included online. However, space is limited on window stickers, so include only the most relevant information.

Quick Response (QR) Codes are a growing trend being used by savvy dealers for on-the-lot vehicle merchandising. QR codes are two-dimensional bar codes containing a variety of information. By scanning a QR code, consumers can be directed to a website, phone number, SMS text message, scheduled calendar event or even business cards.

Dealers should include QR codes on vehicle window stickers; they are free. QR codes allow shoppers to view websites, videos and pictures right on the lot from a mobile device. The possibilities are endless for dealers that recognize local consumers are on their lot when the store is closed.

GETTING STARTED

In vehicle merchandising, dealers should examine dealership culture, personnel and organizational structures to determine levels of involvement. For dealers unable to invest in in-house efforts to merchandise their vehicles, outsourcing options are available.

Outsourcing saves payroll and camera equipment expense. If undecided, an interesting alternative is the hybrid approach, where dealers do most of the work themselves but have a company "catch them up" when they fall behind. Whatever choice the dealer makes, the most important thing is that the job gets done well.

Effective vehicle merchandising is one of the most important time and financial investments dealers can make. With so much capital in vehicle inventory, dealers cannot afford merchandising strategies that present cars poorly, at the wrong prices, and with very few consumer eyeballs. Here is a short list of action items for dealers to employ right away for more effective vehicle merchandising.

ACTION ITEMS

1. *Purchase a high-quality digital SLR camera with wide-angle lens and tripod, or make sure your vendor has this equipment.*

2. *Develop a detailed plan for the pictures and videos capturing your vehicles.*

3. *Ensure your inventory management and website vendor allows detailed vehicle descriptions that are highly searchable.*

4. *Commit to writing detailed marketing descriptions for each vehicle listed online.*

5. *Choose a vehicle merchandising solution that offers pricing analytics and robust, real-time inventory syndication.*

6. *Don't underestimate the power of on-the-lot merchandising. Market effectively to shoppers visiting your store.*

About George

George Nenni is the Vice President of Operations for Dominion Dealer Solutions. George began his automotive career with Dealer Specialties in 1993. He was the Director of Operations for Dealer Specialties when Dominion acquired the business in late 1999 and became the Vice President and General Manager in 2001, first at Dealer Specialties and then at Dominion Dealer Solutions. Today, George oversees Dealer Specialties sales and operations, as well as overall operations for Dominion Dealer Solutions.

George graduated from the Farmer School of Business at Miami University (Oxford, Ohio) with a BS degree in marketing. He and his family live in Middletown, Ohio.

CHAPTER 2

The Premature Death of SEO

By Brian Pasch

A digital marketing strategy would not be complete without a plan for search engine optimization (SEO), which generates organic website traffic. Automotive SEO strategies are designed to get dealer-branded assets on page one of search results without a pay-per-click charge.

A perfect example that demonstrates the power of automotive SEO strategy occurred during the Cash for Clunkers program, also known as the Car Allowance Rebate System (CARS). It was the US government's program to give consumers virtual cash vouchers for trading in an old vehicle. The CARS program dominated media channels and flooded dealers with traffic and questions.

Unfortunately, dealers did not have many answers to give; they were being fed little information themselves. In fact, dealers were worried about how quickly the government would be able to pay them. Some dealers even decided to limit the number of trade-ins they would accept. It was a stressful time for dealers because of the unknown financial liabilities generated from not following the program rules, which no one understood.

In hindsight, the CARS program was hastily implemented. It was a chaotic three months for dealers, from June 2009 until the program ended in August. Before the frenzy started, Dave Wilson, a successful dealer principal who leads the Preston Automotive Group in Maryland, encouraged me to look into this program. Dave was confident Cash for Clunkers would be a great opportunity for internet marketing. Dave was more than right; it would be an amazing case study on the power of SEO strategies.

I purchased the domain www.CashForClunkersFacts.com and posted all the latest news about the CARS program. I made sure all the pages were perfectly formatted, tagged and linked. I created forums to start discussions with consumers and people responded. I added a lead form on the website to connect consumers with dealers.

The site quickly because the No. 1 website on Google page one, under the official government website. The website generated millions of page views and thousands of consumer sales leads. All the traffic was generated organically, not through paid search. Being first to act with a website that matched the search behavior of consumers was the first step. Having content that engaged the consumer was the second step. The combination was unprecedented free traffic, which generated significant revenue by generating leads that could be sold to dealers.

Over the years, search engines have changed the formulas that determine how websites or external content are ranked on page one. Some critics are saying traditional SEO is dead, but I contend that there are always ways to enhance website visibility organically. My passion to leverage the search engines for organic search visibility has never been greater. Increase the challenge, and I respond with new ideas and strategies that help dealers get their media on page one!

Is organic content optimization important? In the graph below, organic traffic to this BMW dealer website represented more than 50 percent of the total traffic to their website.

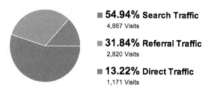

■ **54.94%** Search Traffic
4,867 Visits

■ **31.84%** Referral Traffic
2,820 Visits

■ **13.22%** Direct Traffic
1,171 Visits

Example BMW Dealer Website
Organic Traffic is 54.94%

In recent days, Google representatives have implied that overly optimized websites could be penalized in search results. Rest assured that this warning does not apply to the majority of dealers. Dealership websites for the most part are authentic online marketing portals that provide value to consumers.

If there is one criticism about dealership websites, it is that they lack original, engaging content. And for the dealers that create engaging content, it is not uncommon to see that the content is not optimized for search. Content optimization can be easily fixed through the strategies and tactics shared in this chapter.

When a search engine displays a result, the page content is broken down into three sections: paid search results, organic search results and business directories (see the chart below). Paid search is commonly called search engine marketing (SEM), and each time the advertisement is clicked, the advertiser is charged a fee.

Automotive SEO strategies are designed to increase the likelihood that a dealership website, video, blog or social media profiles appear on page one of organic search results for keywords associated with car research or purchasing funnels for sales and service. Dealership videos, articles, blogs, and photos are generally referred to as their online "content."

SEO tactics are often broken into two categories: on-site and off-site strategies. On-site strategies are tactics that are implemented directly on a dealership website. Off-site strategies generate in-bound links, traffic and social relevance directed toward the dealership's website. The original foundations of on-site SEO included well-written (quality) content on website pages that included keywords in the body of the page text, title tags, subheading tags, and also in the HTML META tags. HTML stands for hyper text markup language, the programming language used to create website pages.

HTML coding is often the responsibility of a dealer's automotive website provider or content writer. If you have no idea what HTML means for your business, *don't panic*. Dealers only need to know that someone who has the HTML training has properly inspected the dealership website and given it a clean bill of health.

Many experts state that Google has diminished the SEO value of the META "keyword" and "description" tags. However, Google does track the occurrences of duplicate page titles and META description tags on your website pages. If it wasn't important, why would they alert webmasters of duplication errors?

On-site SEO tactics should be included in your overall website marketing strategy but no longer do they influence search results as they once did. In fact, many dealership websites are coming out of the box fairly well optimized and only need a small investment in customized tagging.

SEO Tip: Inspect Your Website Page Titles

To make sure your website page titles are SEO-friendly, open a search engine window and type the word "site," followed by your website URL. For example, if your website is www.dealer-seo.com, you would type into the search box: site:http://www.dealer-seo.com. This will allow you to see all the pages on your site so you can see what the pages are called, their titles and the summaries.

Most dealership websites lack an off-site SEO strategy. Quality content development and link building from respected third-party websites is an investment that dealers must include in their marketing budgets.

Quality content will have different meanings to different people, so when you are reviewing website content (articles, videos, photos), ask yourself these questions:

- Would I find this content useful?

- Would someone share this content with a friend?

- Does this content support my brand message or unique selling proposition?

Dealers are advised to stay away from companies that have offers that seem too good to be true. Hundreds of offshore companies are promising page-one placement guaranteed for a few hundred dollars a month. Dealers should seek out companies that work specifically in the automotive industry and that have positive reviews from other dealers.

SEO Tip: Find Highly Rated Marketing Partners
A good source for automotive vendor reviews from actual dealership votes is: www.DrivingSales.com/ratings.
This website is a respected product review source and an educational resource for car dealers.

Generic link farms and shady link exchange platforms are being systematically eliminated from search results. They no longer offer any value to dealerships and should be avoided. Google has publicly commented that companies with websites that are overly optimized or that participate in non-compliant (also known as "black hat") SEO strategies could be penalized. This policy is strong motivation for dealers to make sure their current website is compliant with best-practice (also known as "white hat") SEO strategies.

INVEST IN A WEBSITE AUDIT

Dealers should request an independent audit of their website from a qualified professional to ensure that the on-site SEO tactics are in compliance with industry best practices. The checklist for on-site SEO compliance should verify that:

- Pages have a unique page title.

- Pages have a unique HTML META description tag.

- Pages are written to engage real people and are not overly optimized with keywords appearing in every paragraph, making reading awkward and clumsy.

- Pages do not have hidden text or keyword-stuffing techniques.

- Pages are included in your site map and are being indexed by the search engines.

- Photos are properly labeled with ALT tags.

- Hyperlinks in the text are designed to aid in navigation and research, and are not overly optimized for just keywords.

- The website has Google Analytics and Webmaster Tools installed with registered site maps for web pages and another for videos.

- The website does not have numerous 404 errors, which are pages no longer found by Google.

- Videos posted on your website are included in a video site map.

An off-site SEO audit includes documenting the number of in-bound links, online reviews, appearance in online business directories, and basic search visibility for a dealership website. A comprehensive SEO review is in the dealer's best interests since organic search traffic is a significant portion of overall website visits.

IS CHANGE HAPPENING TOO FAST?

SEO strategies have been impacted by changes in how search engines display keyword search results. If you are a student of search marketing, you will agree that the pace at which Google has changed search results is much faster than most business owners can update their digital marketing strategies.

Google has given marketers some insights on what influences their search algorithm; Yahoo and Bing have been mostly silent on the matter. Google has indicated that its algorithm is influenced by social media signals (votes), which has forced SEO strategists to educate dealers on the importance of online engagement.

Dealers are still divided on how to engage with consumers using social media. The debate, however, is not whether social "likes" or relevance can impact search priority on Google. Peer behavior is more a factor in Google search rankings than ever before. Google's stance is that social signals make their search engine results more relevant for users and less likely to be "gamed" by black-hat SEO companies.

One example is Google+, which has already demonstrated its power to appear on page one of search results, despite being a new social media platform. Dealers looking to increase local search visibility should create a free Google+ profile for their dealership. Once created, an investment should be made to post engaging content on Google+ and to create a process to invite customers into the dealership's "circle."

ONLINE REPUTATION SCORES IMPACT SEO

The evolution of online business directories has a direct impact on SEO strategies. Business listings are now prominently displayed on page one for popular broad keyword searches like "used cars" or "Ford dealers." Search for "Chevrolet Dealers" in Google, Yahoo and Bing, and each display their own directory listings on page one. Google and Yahoo business listings also show reviews.

Online business directories with consumer review data have now married internet reputation management (IRM) processes to effective SEO strategies.

Any business that is displayed on page one with low or negative reviews can actually reduce the number of leads, calls and traffic generated from a search engine. Dealers looking to better understand the importance of online reviews will be pleased to know that there is a complete chapter on this very subject (see "Online Reviews and Moldy Hotels").

SEO Tip: Inspect Your Online Reviews

Open a Google search box, type in the name of a dealership, and add the word "review." For example, if the dealership name is Edmund Hyundai, you would search "Edmond Hyundai Reviews."

Click on the listings that appear on page one of search results to quickly inspect reviews on websites that have been optimized for the dealership name.

Since online reviews will impact the organic click-through results to a dealership website, there must be a process inside the dealership to inspect and discuss review counts and quality each month.

A simple spreadsheet that tracks dealership reviews across the top 10 review websites could be a powerful tool to ensure your reviews are supporting your SEO efforts. Discuss the spreadsheet at weekly or monthly management meetings. If needed, align management compensation plans to include improvements in online review counts and scores.

Websites that could be included in a review-tracking spreadsheet are Google Places, DealerRater.com, Edmunds.com, Yelp.com, Cars.com, Yahoo Local, Bing Local, AngiesList.com, CitySearch.com, Judysbook. com, YellowPages.com, and CarDealerSale.com.

VIDEO ENGAGEMENT ENHANCES PAGE-ONE RESULTS

With YouTube being the second most popular search engine in the world, an SEO strategy would not be complete today if it did not include video. Dealers are just starting to realize that videos can communicate their unique selling proposition and assist consumers in making educated decisions about the cars they sell and service.

Video messages are easily communicated on mobile devices and for consumers on the go. Have you ever tried to read a website page while traveling in the back of a taxi? If you have visited CNN.com lately, you will notice a growing percentage of stories are presented in video form. Don't swim upstream; embrace video with passion.

Search engines are designed to reward the click preferences of consumers. Search engine users can absorb information faster via video, so the search engines often include video thumbnails or links on page one.

Dealers who seek an Unfair Advantage must invest in video production to connect with more in-market consumers.

SEO Tip: Be First in Market With Video
Aggressive dealers should be the first in their market to provide compelling walk-around videos for all new models they sell as soon as they arrive in the showroom.

Dealers can leapfrog the competition by filming their videos at auto shows where new models are on display months before they arrive in the dealer showroom. Search engines often reward being "first" for unique content, so what are you waiting for? This is another example why reading this book will give you an Unfair Advantage in the marketplace.

If you are questioning the power of video in your SEO strategy, open a Google search box, enter "2013 Mazda CX-5 Minneapolis," and see what appears at the top on page-one organic results. At the time of this writing, the video produced by Morries Mazda has more than 48,000 views, and it was only 90 days old. (For specific tactical advice and strategies on video SEO, please read full discussion in "The Biggest Blunder" chapter.)

Automotive SEO strategies are best summarized as the marriage of compelling content, natural link building, social media engagement and video marketing. Together these tactics can increase the organic traffic to a dealership website.

Vendor partners that do not communicate with each other may complicate the coordination of multifaceted digital and social media strategies. In most cases, the dealer principal or general manager does not have sufficient training to coordinate search-marketing strategies without help.

SEO ACTION ITEMS

Here is a summary of actions that dealers and marketing professionals can incorporate into their SEO strategies:

- Check the dealership website for basic SEO compliance, which includes unique page titles, well-formed URLs, and unique META description tags.

- Develop a list of the top 10 keywords that the dealership wants to target for page-one visibility.

- Create optimized pages on the dealership website for each keyword goal.

- Create and publish optimized videos for each keyword goal.

- Develop an off-site linking strategy for the dealership's content.

- Implement a social media engagement strategy to increase Google +1 votes, Facebook likes, and Twitter posts for dealership online assets.

About Brian

Brian Pasch, CEO of PCG Digital Marketing, has built his business insights and strategy on a foundation consisting of more than 20 years of information technology and marketing leadership. His career history includes work in the public sector, senior telecom analyst on Wall Street, and an incredible talent for building successful, private enterprises.

Fresh out of Rutgers University, Brian published his first book and software package with Prentice Hall in 1984. Since that time he has been recognized as a builder of world-class data warehousing models, a creator of award-winning search marketing strategies, and the highest-rated Internet Trainer in the automotive industry.

Recognizing a powerful shift in corporate advertising spending, Pasch founded PCG Digital Marketing in 2005 to assist growing companies with their digital marketing strategy. Brian's ability to speak authoritatively to business leaders and their technical teams on business architecture, marketing and sales helped catapult their growth and credibility.

In August 2011, *Inc.* magazine named PCG Digital Marketing the 192nd Fastest-Growing Private Company in the United States. PCG was also ranked in the Top 10 Fastest-Growing Private Companies in New Jersey where PCG is based. PCG serves many industries, but their largest by far is the automotive retail industry where they serve hundreds of car dealerships across the US and Canada.

Brian Pasch is an avid writer and blogger, and his commentary on search engine optimization and digital marketing can be easily found on the internet. In 2012, he founded PCG Consulting to provide vendor-neutral advice to business leaders looking to create a comprehensive marketing strategy that includes the latest opportunities in traditional, digital and social media.

Brian is an active speaker at automotive industry conferences, 20 Groups and digital marketing workshops. His popular training programs make him an in-demand speaker with elite flying status. Brian is an advocate of balanced living and takes time to invest in his health and spiritual well being. That lifestyle includes making time for his family and friends in New Jersey where he lives by the Jersey Shore.

CHAPTER 3

The Biggest Blunder: Ignoring Video Marketing

By AJ LeBlanc

Have you watched a video on your tablet, mobile device or laptop recently? The exponential growth of online video usage is a huge opportunity for business owners and marketing companies.

Despite the rise in market share captured by online video websites, car dealers have had a lukewarm response to the investment needed to create a dominant online video strategy. Dealers must re-evaluate their reluctance to creating a powerful set of video messages for their dealership. Ignoring video will be a historic blunder!

YouTube.com is the second largest search engine, yet few dealers have leveraged its consumer reach. For example, dealers reading this book may be first hearing about the YouTube Promoted Video Program (PVP)? Dealers seeking an Unfair Advantage in video will see the benefits of having their video messages promoted on page one of YouTube, if the message is on the mark.

PVP is similar to Google Adwords in that for a fee it will promote any video to the top of "page one" search results on YouTube. Dealers are charged when the video is clicked and watched. You may be the first in your market to leverage this ad platform, but you must have a unique video strategy to make this work. This chapter will give you ideas on which videos can work for your brand and market.

TV COMMERCIALS DO *NOT* CONSTITUTE AN ONLINE VIDEO STRATEGY

Many dealers have an existing strategy to be dominant on radio, cable TV or in print. However, republishing cable TV commercials on YouTube, Vimeo, or any number of search engines does not constitute a unique online video marketing strategy.

An online video strategy for dealers must have broader messaging that matches the keywords that consumers are researching. The video campaign should include clips that reinforce the dealership's branding.

Branding videos have a longer lifespan and effective reach when compared to a video highlighting a 30-day sale. I don't know how you feel, but seeing videos in search results that are old TV commercials from last year reflect poorly on the dealership. Dealers must create timeless videos to promote service, parts and used car sales, which are profitable business units that demand additional sales volume. Will you deliver those leads that are within your reach?

VIDEO BY THE NUMBERS

Why should you invest in a video strategy? Dealers who seek an Unfair Advantage must have the right tools in their toolbox to dominate their competition online—video is a powerful tool.

Data collected by eMarketer.com and published on HubSpot.com shared the following statistics on internet video:

- Online video viewers will reach 169.3 million in 2012.

- 53.5 percent of the population and 70.8 percent of internet users (up 7.1 percent from 2011) will watch online videos in 2012.

- Mobile video viewers will reach 54.6 million in 2012.

- Smartphone video viewers will reach 51.2 million in 2012.

If that wasn't enough evidence, online video ads were ranked the most useful ad format over all other digital and traditional mediums according to the "Auto Shopper Behavior Study" conducted by Google and Compete.com in 2011. Paid search advertisements (SEM) came in just behind video.

For car dealers, videos allow the unique selling proposition and dealership brand to be mobile; untethered from their primary website. Videos can be effectively placed on a dealership website, but they also "travel" the internet as independent marketing tools.

Similar to the organic content strategies shared in the automotive SEO chapter, video SEO strategies are designed to bring your "live" message to consumers who are researching or shopping online without paying per view. You may be surprised just how visible videos can be on page one of search results.

In the example shown below, if a consumer was searching Google for an Acura repair center near Chicago and typed into the search engine "Acura Auto Repair Chicago," McGrath Acura is the only dealer to appear on page one of search results with a video.

Why is this significant? Videos that appear on page one of search results have significantly higher click rates when compared to regular text listings. The more videos a dealership has strategically published to appear in search engine results pages (SERP), the more they'll increase the connection of their brand message, website address and phone number to consumers.

STARTING YOUR VIDEO STRATEGY

The opportunities for video marketing and SEO are virtually unlimited and can support all profit centers in the dealership. Dealers that want to influence consumers while they're using search engines to research cars, auto service, loans, leases, or special finance can connect with video and communicate their willingness to serve.

In the book *Winning the Zero Moment of Truth* by Jim Lecinski of Google, he shares research data that shows that car shoppers will interact with more than 18 different online sources and websites before contacting a dealership. The period of time is called the Zero Moment of Truth, or ZMOT. Video marketing and video SEO are powerful strategies to connect with consumers before they make a decision to contact a local dealer.

Before you start video production, you should review your current marketing and branding strategy to ensure your online messaging is consistent with your offline message. For example, if you're a one-price dealership, your online videos shouldn't be giving conflicting messages on price.

Second, each video should have a defined objective; what's the desired outcome after a consumer watches the video. Do you want the consumer to call? Complete an application? Email for additional information or visit a website? By having a clear, desired outcome, your script can reinforce the desired call to action.

Be realistic about your ability to script, film, edit and publish your videos. In this chapter, I'll share how you can optimize any video to appear in search results for reasonable local keyword goals. With that in mind, do you want a poor quality video viewed thousands of times when a small investment could produce a higher quality product?

Once your videos are published, you'll want to review your website analytics as well as the video analytics provided on each video platform. Popular video sites like YouTube, Vimeo, Viddler, and VodPod all provide some form of viewing statistics.

However, what counts as a video "view" will vary on each website platform. A view may not be triggered unless the majority of the video is watched. Dealers that have properly optimized videos with links to their website in the video description area will also need to look at how many referral visitors are coming directly. These clicks are valuable regardless of how much of the video was actually watched.

VIDEO STRATEGIES FOR NEW AND USED CARS

Video can be created to increase the visibility of individual new and used cars that are in stock at a dealership. The goal for these videos, when properly optimized, is to connect with consumers that are searching for year, make and model in their local communities. These videos contain actual photos or videos of the vehicle along with an audio track that's customized for each dealership.

Services are available that download dealership inventory data and static photos to create videos that showcase the vehicle much better that a static slideshow. The automated voice-over process takes the burden off the dealership to create dozens or hundreds of walk-around videos each month. Completed videos are published by video SEO service providers to multiple video search engines. The automated services increase reach and frequency by eliminating the tedious labor involved with high-volume dealerships.

Dealers that want a more customized approach to video marketing their inventory can take their own videos and load the final cut to popular video websites. It's becoming easier for dealers to film their own videos using compact HD cameras and mobile applications like cDemo Mobile Inspector, which run on Apple iOS and Android mobile operating systems.

VIDEO SEO FOR NEW AND USED CAR SEARCHES

In the example below, you'll see just how "visible" well-optimized vehicle videos appear in search results. In fact, the first two organic results shown for this Google search are videos.

If a consumer was looking for a 2010 Jeep Wrangler, the video options are more colorful, visible and compelling to click. So how did these videos get ranked so well for this search phrase?

OPTIMIZING VIDEOS FOR SEARCH

To upload a video on sites like YouTube, you're required to complete a few important data fields. How these fields are completed influences how the search engines display videos.

Keep in mind that search engines aren't translating the audio track on the video to determine its message. The search engines have to use the titles, description and tag provided by the person loading the video.

To maximize the chances a video appears in search results for specific keyword goals, the keyword should appear in the video title and description. Shorter, more direct video titles work best.

Before loading a video, review this optimization checklist.

✓ Video content should be unique.

✓ Don't load the same video twice on the same website.

✓ Video length should be less than two minutes to keep viewers' attention.

✓ Upload your video to multiple video sites. Don't put eggs in one basket/network.

✓ Optimize video title, tags, categories, descriptions and location to match your keyword goals.

✓ Hyperlink website URL, phone numbers, store address, maps when possible in the description area of the video.

✓ Proper keyword optimization shouldn't read as "spam" to the search engines.

VIDEO SEO FOR FIXED OPERATIONS

Videos can be created to enhance online visibility for vehicle service and maintenance offered by dealers, including oil changes, brakes, tires, transmission service, fluid changes and air conditioning systems.

Dealers that want to compete with national service chains can showcase their superior facilities, competitive rates, and experienced staff extremely well using video. Whose lounge and bathroom would you rather use while waiting for an oil change?

Present the facts in separate videos so the videos can be optimized for popular keywords used by consumers searching for companies to service their car. For example, a Hyundai dealer located in Pasadena that wanted to increase it's online visibility for service could upload a video that's optimized for the keyword phrase "Hyundai Mechanic Pasadena" as shown below:

VIDEO SEO FOR CONQUEST STRATEGIES

Dealers are becoming accustomed to creating videos to promote their brand. Dealers that seek an Unfair Advantage should create videos to conquest franchise dealers in their market. Conquest videos are optimized to appear on the first page of search results for models that compete with those a dealer sells. This is an untapped opportunity for creative dealers.

Let's imagine a Kia dealer in Appleton, Wisconsin, that believes that a consumer considering a Hyundai Sonata will also consider a Kia Optima. The dealer creates a video that compares the Kia Optima to the Hyundai Sonata and highlights why the Kia is a better vehicle. The video closes with a call to action—a no-obligation test-drive comparison.

Once the video is completed, it can be loaded on to sites like YouTube and optimized to show in search results when consumers are shopping for a Hyundai Sonata in the dealer's local market.

The video title can be "Kia Optima Vs. Hyundai Sonata – Appleton,

WI" Conquest video SEO expands the keywords that a dealership video program can attack because there are hundreds of popular car models searched each day. Before creating dozens of videos, dealers should select a few models to test with this conquest strategy.

CREATING A COMPREHENSIVE VIDEO STRATEGY

It's clear that the search engines favor video content in search result pages. Providing compelling videos for in-market consumers has to be part of a marketing strategy that seeks to dominate the market. Dealers that don't have the internal resources to create professional quality videos should hire a partner that will deliver the right content at the right price.

Delaying video engagement isn't a choice when you consider the reach, frequency and quality that messaging videos can deliver in search and social media challenges.

About AJ

AJ LeBlanc is the Managing Partner of Car-mercial.com, a digital marketing company that created a proprietary software platform that leads the automotive industry in video search engine optimization (SEO). AJ LeBlanc is a frequent contributor to industry publications, including *Auto Success*, *Dealer Marketing Magazine*, and *Canadian Auto Dealer* magazine.

AJ is a popular conference and 20 Group speaker, leading workshop presentations on video marketing and optimization. His automotive conference participation includes Digital Dealer, Digital Marketing Strategies Conference (DMSC), Automotive Boot Camp, and PCG Pit Stops.

AJ and his team at Car-mercial launched CarBuyersEngine.com in 2011, the first video search portal in the automotive industry. The Car-Mercial.com software platform produces, optimizes, distributes and manages videos for first-page rankings of popular search phrases for car dealers' brands and markets.

AJ was born in New Haven, Connecticut, and raised in Vero Beach, Florida. He received his MBA from National University in San Diego and currently resides in South Florida.

CHAPTER 4

Digital Advertising: How to Get More Traffic Right Now

By Brian Pasch

"I want more leads, and I need them now!" The plea came from a general manger who was frustrated with the volume of leads his website generated. So I took out my book of marketing spells to find the right incantation. I recited the words verbatim that unlock immediate traffic to any website. I closed the book. The manager looked at me with awe and asked, "Is that it? Will my traffic increase tomorrow?" I smiled, "Sure, as long as we set up that Google Adwords account this afternoon!"

Digital advertising on the internet comes in many forms: search engine marketing (SEM), display advertising and video advertising. SEM refers to advertising on search engines only. Digital advertising can generate immediate traffic to a dealership website, but I must also add a warning. Traffic generated by digital advertising to a dealer's website should be part of a conversion strategy. The traffic and landing page should be optimized to generate a lead or phone call.

Some marketers' use the term pay per click (PPC) interchangeably with SEM. Digital advertising campaigns can be billed on a cost per click (CPC), cost per impression, (CPM), and cost per view (CPV).

A perfect example of impression-based billing is banner advertising. Local radio, TV, or newspaper websites, for example, may invoice advertisers not on banner clicks but on how many times the banner has been displayed to a visitor, which is called an impression. Online advertising rate cards are often priced in cost per thousand impressions (CPM).

Banner advertising can also be billed on a per-click basis; the Google Display Network (GDN) is one example. In fact, many car dealers prefer to run banner advertising campaigns on a per-click basis because it aligns the digital advertising costs to their end goal: to entice qualified traffic to their website.

> **Paid Search Vocabulary**
> Advertising campaigns can be billed on a *cost per click (CPC)*, *cost per impression (CPM)*, and *cost per view (CPV)*.

Regardless of which billing method is selected, paid advertising on search engines, websites, or mobile devices is best described as targeted "traffic now" investments, a term coined by author Dennis Galbraith. Unlike search engine optimization (SEO) or social media, website traffic generated by SEM is immediate.

SEM generates highly targeted traffic from ready-to-buy consumers using a search engine. Its impact lasts as long as the marketing campaigns are funded. When funding runs out, online ads no longer appear.

Some critics of paid search take the position that a website that has strong organic visibility, derived from an investment in SEO and social media, generates an annuity of traffic and leads at a very low cost. These critics have decided that they don't need to run SEM campaigns like Google Adwords.

I respect the passionate stance of these critics, as a former SEO zealot myself, however, consumers frequently use broad keywords in their searches like "used cars," "Toyota sale," "F150," "Camaro prices," or "Hyundai dealers." Aside from business directory listings like Google Places, a local dealer would have difficulty appearing at the top of page one for any of these phrases. SEO is helpful when consumers add a local city to their search phrase, like "Chicago Hyundai dealers."

> ### SEM Vocabulary
> *Broad keywords* are one- or two-word searches like "Mazda Dealer." *Long-tail keywords* are those with three or more words like "2012 Honda Civic Sale." *Geo-targeted keywords* are those with a city, state or county like "Napa Valley Honda Dealer."

Other critics consider paid search "expensive" compared to other forms of advertising and have decided to eliminate it from their budgets. These dealers have a significant portion of their budget allocated to some combination of radio, cable TV, newspaper, billboards and direct mail. After reviewing hundreds of dealer budgets, those that are overweighted with traditional media investments are the most prone to seeing declining market share of new online shoppers coming to their website.

Dealers using paid search believe they can increase the exposure of their inventory to in-market consumers at an affordable cost. Are they correct?

From my research, the average cost to get a consumer to visit a dealership website using Google Adwords is between $1.30 to $1.90 a click. I also found that the average cost to generate a visitor to a dealership website from any combination of radio, TV and newspaper was $16 per visitor.

SEM campaigns can generate eight times more website traffic than the same dollars invested in traditional media. That's great news if that's important to the dealer's overall marketing strategy. I'm not saying that sarcastically because today I still meet dealers who are convinced that investing 80 to 90 percent of their marketing budget offline is what's making them successful.

Despite the ability for paid search to drive qualified traffic at a lower cost than traditional media, most dealers are underfunding their SEM campaigns. Some aren't investing in paid search at all. This is a wakeup call for dealers that aren't using paid search in their marketing strategies.

> ### Budget Tip
> There's money in the dealership budget for paid search! Reallocate 10 to 15 percent of current traditional media investments and watch how much traffic and leads are generated from an optimized SEM campaign.

I want to be clear; I'm not implying that dealers shouldn't be investing in traditional media. There's a distinct limit on how much traffic can be generated from paid search. That limit is dependent on local market competition, population, and the creativity of the campaign setup. Paid search is only part of a comprehensive marketing strategy; it's not optional.

When executed properly, traditional media is a valuable part of a comprehensive marketing strategy. There are chapters in this book that communicate the power of traditional media and branding, so I'll let the experts outline a winning strategy.

As an advocate for digital advertising investments, my recommendations, as based on results from paid search and banner campaigns, are set up properly. Advertising platforms like Google Adwords aren't a "set it and forget it" magic bullet. Paid search investments need weekly review, refinements and a testing discipline to ensure optimal conversion rates are achieved.

SETTING YOUR DIGITAL ADVERTISING GOALS

Before starting a digital advertising investment, someone needs to be in charge of the overall goal of the campaigns. The overall goal may be to sell more cars or promote your fixed ops department, but there are many different ways to tackle these objectives via digital advertising.

In general, there are two major types of campaign goals: lead generation, also known as direct response, and brand awareness or branding. You should understand the difference between the two goals before you launch your campaign.

For a lead-generation campaign, it's best to have a tangible incentive for the consumer in mind, such as a cash rebate, coupon or gas card. The best method to deliver lead generation is by understanding what motivates the in-market consumer, and advertising that incentive via targeted search ads and targeted banner ads.

A brand awareness campaign gives you the opportunity to connect with the consumer on another level, and while they may not be ready to buy now, it's your job to have them consider your dealership in the future. It's important to understand that the calculation of return on investment

(ROI) will be more difficult to calculate for brand awareness than for a direct response campaign.

You can deliver this branding message via broader "Honda dealer" type searches, remarketing banners and video advertising. You should align all forms of advertising with this message.

In constructing your dealership's "branding hook" or "value proposition," you need to let consumers know why they should pick your dealership over your competitors. Are you known for a hassle-free buying process? Or do you have the largest inventory in the state? These are questions you need to address before you pay for advertising space in a YouTube pre-roll, or on a premium content publisher like CNBC.

HOW PAID SEARCH WORKS

In its simplest form, SEM based on keyword searches on a search engine consists of the following elements:

- *Accounts:* Accounts are normally associated with a credit card for billing purposes. If you had three stores that wanted to use separate credit cards for monthly billing, three accounts would need to be created.

- *Campaigns:* Campaigns are primarily segregated to allocate funds appropriately to each campaign effort (i.e., new cars, used cars, service, parts), and also to target separate devices and geographic areas.

- *Ad groups:* Inside each campaign, ad groups are created. Dealers often desire to target specific models of cars or services, and ad groups can be created to achieve that goal. For example, inside a new car campaign, a Honda dealer could have ad groups setup for Honda Accord, Honda Civic, Honda Odyssey, etc. Ad groups are used to align specific ad copy targeted at a tightly themed group of keywords to keep relevance between keyword, ad copy, and landing page as tight as possible. This contributes to the optimization efforts, increasing quality score and reducing CPC.

- *Keywords:* Inside each ad group, there are keywords that you consider related to the marketing goals of this department.

For example, in the Service Ad Group, a dealer could include keywords such as "oil change," "discount tires," "brake service" or "wheel alignment." Keyword match settings can be fine-tuned with "exact match" only or to include broader match or even negative matches.

- *Ads:* Inside each ad group are ads that are triggered when consumers type in a matching keyword. Ads can be in different formats and sizes: text ads, banner ads for display advertising on desktops and tablets, banner ads for mobile, and video ads. Each ad can be associated with specific keywords for added granularity. Display and video have a completely different way of being targeted.

- *Landing pages:* Landing pages are the website pages that are displayed to consumers when they click the ad. For most dealers, the landing page is part of the main dealership website. Ads should direct consumers to pages that reinforce the advertising message. Landing pages should serve a purpose!

- *Target audience:* All digital advertising campaigns allow the advertiser to select the cities where the paid ads will be displayed. The campaign parameters can also exclude certain hours of the day(s) in the week or increase bids during certain hours. Advanced campaigns using display and video can also target consumers based on a limited set of demographics.

It pays to make sure that their important parameters are clearly defined before an SEM campaign is started. A dealer selling new Honda Civics in New Jersey would have little success if their paid search ads were being displayed to consumers in Orange County, California.

The advertising coverage map is unique to the dealer's marketing goals, local competition and population density. A dealer in Manhattan may limit their marketing radius to 25 miles whereas a dealer in Utah may expand their radius to over 100 miles.

SEM Tip

Inspect the target audience settings in the SEM campaign. Too often the parameters aren't aligned with the dealer's marketing goals.

LANDING PAGES ARE CLICK DESTINATIONS

If a text or banner advertisement spoke about the 2013 Mazda CX-5, the landing page should be optimized to present the CX-5 with a call to action. A landing page is where a consumer is taken when they click on your paid advertisement.

Landing pages should have a call to action, which could be to schedule a test drive, to download a brochure, join a membership program, receive $1,000 cash-back on trade-in, service coupons or special incentives. Taking the consumer to the home page of a dealership website is a wasted investment. SEM campaigns should make it easier for consumers to be connected with the promotion stated in the ad.

SEM strategists have suggested that PPC ads shouldn't click through to the dealership website because typical landing pages aren't optimized for conversion. Specifically, the inability to turn off the navigation bars on landing pages creates too many distractions and lures the consumers' eyes away from the primary message. Additionally, most platforms don't present the vehicle search with a clear call to action or *lead form*.

While this is true, few dealers or vendors provide adequate resources to quickly create, modify and maintain dozens of off-site landing pages that are optimized for conversion. As dealers understand the potential of SEM, they'll pursue companies that specialize on conversion optimization because without optimized landing pages, SEM campaigns are inefficient.

IT'S ALL ABOUT CONVERSION—ALMOST!

Once paid search campaigns are started, data is collected and reports can be generated to see which keywords and ads are creating the best "desired results." The desired results may vary per dealer, but normally success is measured by conversion—the number of calls, chats, downloads or lead-form submissions that are generated.

Digital Advertising Vocabulary

An *offline conversion* occurs when someone calls your dealership after clicking a paid ad. An *online conversion* occurs when someone submits an email lead after clicking a paid ad.

To measure conversion, tracking phone numbers are needed on landing pages. About half the "conversions" today on dealership SEM campaigns are phone calls. Despite the obvious desire for consumers to pick up the phone and call, less than half of paid search campaigns have been set up to properly track phone conversions. Conversion code also needs to be installed on all website forms, which is often omitted as well.

These two common omissions make a case that dealers should either invest in additional training or outsource the campaign management to a certified partner. Dealers looking at upgrading to a new website provider should ask specific questions about the platform's ability to properly track SEM calls and leads.

> **SEM Tip**
> Do not start a paid search campaign until your staff or vendor partner has secured conversion tracking for leads and phone calls.

With conversion tracking installed, dealers should expect a monthly review of click costs, costs per lead, and a number of other campaign statistics that are valuable to understand.

Dealers should inspect the ad groups and keywords that are generating conversions at both the high and low end of the "cost per lead" spectrum when a few months of data has been collected. Dealers should be involved in the monthly SEM because their knowledge of the business can help direct budgets and strategy.

AD COPY AND KEYWORD CHOICES

A case in point was a Google Adwords campaign that was running at a Honda dealership. I noticed that the parts ad group was spending a large portion of their budget on one keyword: "Honda Parts." At first glance you might not see anything wrong with that keyword, but the conversion rate was very low and CPL high.

After further investigation, the reason why the CPC was high and the conversion was so low was the message in the ad. The ad stated "Discount Honda Parts" and a line about "saving online." The only problem with the ad was that it didn't communicate the Honda dealership's website only sold Honda *automotive* parts.

The high volume of ad clicks was most likely coming from owners of Honda motorcycles, generators and lawnmowers, which resulted in high bounce rates. A "bounce" is when a consumer lands on a website page and immediately leaves without visiting any additional pages. Dealers can hone in on more relevant traffic by using advanced match types on keywords that are in the campaign as well as negative keywords.

The combination of changing ad copy—in this example to "Only Honda Auto Parts"—and refining keywords is an important job for an SEM campaign manager. Dealers should expect to have a report presented by the SEM vendor on what ad copy and keyword changes are being made each month. The most changes will come in the first six months, as keywords and landing pages are tested.

DISPLAY ADVERTISING

Display advertising differs from SEM in that instead of advertising on a search engine, you're buying ad space on other websites such as FoxNews.com, CNBC.com, and other local content publishers and forums, and advertising a graphical banner instead of a text ad.

Also, instead of bidding on keyword searches to target your text ad on a search engine, there are many different ways to target your banner ad. There are two main classifications for display targeting: user-based targeting and placement-based targeting.

User-based targeting is based on information that Google and other data providers know about what websites you've visited and other identifiable information, in accordance with industry regulated privacy restrictions.

The different types of user-based targeting are retargeting or remarketing, which I will explain later in this chapter; behavioral based targeting; and demographic targeting. Behavioral/interest targeting is based on your search and page-view history, and has been classified by Google into biddable audiences, such as vehicle shoppers, and vehicle maintenance. Demographic targeting is simply based on age and gender.

Placement-based targeting is based on the website on which you're buying ad space. There are three types: topic targeting, placement targeting and contextual targeting.

- Topic targeting is bidding on groups of similarly themed

websites, such as BMW, or high-performance vehicle websites.

- Placement targeting is the specific domain that you can either bid on or exclude.

- Contextual targeting is based on a keyword search term. For example, if a dealer were to enter the keyword "Ford F150" in contextual targeting, Google would run a search on its own Google Display Network for that term. It would show the dealer's ads on the GDN that are relevant to the keyword "Ford F150."

RETARGETING MAXIMIZES ALL MARKETING INVESTMENTS

One of the most exciting areas of paid search marketing is called retargeting, also referred to as remarketing. Retargeting allows dealers to leverage existing website traffic that doesn't convert on the first visit. When implemented properly, retargeting will increase the ROI of all marketing investments that drive traffic to a dealer's website.

Retargeting works by placing tracking code in a consumer's browser when they visit the dealership website. When they leave, this tracking code stays in their browser's "memory." When the consumer visits other websites on the internet that have advertising banners, your banner ads will be prioritized and displayed on those websites.

The primary ROI metric to consider for a retargeting campaign is a view-through conversion. A view-through conversion, shown in the illustration below, is when the following sequence of events occurs:

1. A user visits your website and opts into your remarketing audience.

2. That user sees an impression of your ad.

3. That user returns to your website and submits an email lead.

When view-through conversions are used in the calculation of CPL, remarketing campaigns usually achieve a CPL of about $15 to $20.

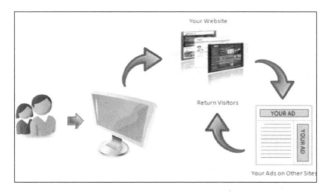

In the example below, a consumer who visits the Prestige Volvo website shopping for a car will also see their banner advertisement on popular websites like Mashable.com. These banner placements don't cost the dealership until the consumer clicks to come back to the Prestige Volvo website.

If you consider this advertising model, dealers can get hundreds of thousands of impressions a month at a very low cost. The Google Display Network (GDN) covers 89 percent of all websites that offer banner advertising. Retargeting networks are also available on Yahoo/ Bing and third-party networks.

On average, a click will cost $2.50, which makes retargeting affordable. If dealers got started with retargeting using the GDN, it's the equivalent of having billboards on 89 percent of all streets in your market.

If you want to increase brand visibility with messages that can be easily changed based on monthly promotions or seasonable messages, dealers who want an Unfair Advantage can no longer ignore this advertising strategy.

VIDEO PRE-ROLL AND PROMOTED VIDEOS

In the chapter on video SEO, AJ LeBlanc shared impressive statistics on the reach and frequency of online video. Since video is the most effective advertising format according to a 2011 study by Google and Compete.com, dealers looking for an Unfair Advantage need to have a paid video marketing strategy in place.

There's two opportunities with paid video search marketing: video pre-roll/post-roll and YouTube.com's Promoted Video Program (PVP). Video pre/post-roll allows your video advertisements to run before or after a consumer plays a video on YouTube.

Readers who have watched videos on popular websites like CNN. com have witnessed firsthand the advertisements that run for 15 or 30 seconds prior to a news story. In the same manner, dealers can use Google Adwords to publish video messages that will play in their local market when consumers watch a video on YouTube.

Keep in mind that YouTube.com is the second largest search engine in the world. YouTube advertising allows dealers to communicate using video to consumers who prefer watching video online. It's the perfect opportunity for dealers who create clever marketing videos that are specifically designed for YouTube viewers.

The second opportunity is the YouTube PVP. This program is similar to Google Adwords in that can promote any video to the top of "page one" search results on YouTube by keyword bids. Dealers are charged when the video is clicked and watched.

In the example below, you'll see that promoted videos appear in the top and can also show on the right column of YouTube search results. The top four organic videos received more than 110,000 views. Any Honda dealer would love to place their walk-around video for a 2012 Honda Accord at the top of this search results page for local consumers to view.

Dealers looking to be omnipresent online cannot afford to miss the hundreds of thousands of YouTube videos presented to local residents every day!

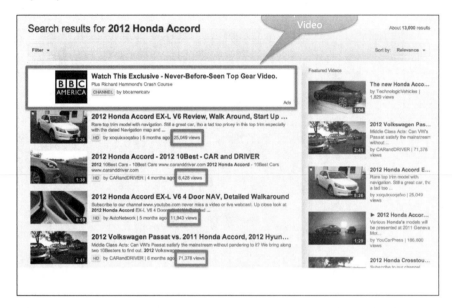

CREATING AN ACTION PLAN FOR DIGITAL ADVERTISING

Dealers looking for that Unfair Advantage in their marketplace cannot ignore the many opportunities offered by digital advertising. Dealers should contact their existing advertising agency or website vendor to discuss expanding their campaigns with the ideas presented in this chapter.

Dealers who aren't currently using digital advertising in their marketing strategy should seek a vendor partner that will ensure that proper conversion tracking (phone call and lead forms) will be installed. Dealers should also review the type of monthly reports that will be presented to ensure that a management discussion can take place based on the data presented.

Most important, dealers should understand the level of customization and support they will receive from their digital advertising vendor. This should include a discussion on who's responsible for creating retargeting banners, how often they can be changed, and how keyword strategies are created and changed over time.

CHAPTER 5

Internet Transparency and Pink Slime

By Brian Pasch

One thing that all dealers share is that the internet has forever changed the automotive retail industry. The transparency introduced by the internet requires dealers to rethink their business operations and marketing strategies. We don't have to go back far to understand the power of the internet in regards to business practice.

For years, the meat packing industry has used Lean Finely Textured Beef (LFTB) as a beef-based food additive for hamburgers. LFTB is an FDA-approved food additive that does not need additional labeling if less than 15 percent is used in beef products.

According to Wikipedia, "The term 'pink slime' was coined in 2002 by Gerald Zirnstein, who at that time was a microbiologist for the U.S. Department of Agriculture (USDA) Food Safety and Inspection Service.

When ABC News broke the story in March 2012, the pink slime videos went viral on the internet. The story created widespread consumer outrage that forced chain supermarkets to stop selling products that contained LFTB. The financial impact to the beef industry was significant, and it was a death-blow to at least one large meat processing plant. The transparency of the internet took practices that were once deemed acceptable but truly "back office" and brought them into the public eye.

THE PINK SLIME IN AUTOMOTIVE RETAILING

Regardless of past successes, dealers who ignore the transparency of the internet will soon find that muscling their way to the top will no longer be quite that easy.

> Are there acceptable business practices at dealerships today that would have the same negative consumer response as pink slime, if placed under the microscope?

Successful dealerships must have a code of ethics and a business vision that clearly understands the power and transparency of the internet. This vision has to shape the way dealers do business. It applies to how dealers estimate trades, price cars, advertise sales, and treat customers in sales and service.

The unified vision has to start at the top of the organization. Any dealer principal that uses the term "Internet Thing" is most likely not seeing the power of the internet. Dealers that do not see how their in-store actions impact future customers are most likely not seeing the true influence that the internet can bear on their multimillion-dollar asset. Dealers need to hold a mirror to their organizational processes and ask themselves, "Is this policy or practice safe for public consumption?"

Just this week, I read an article by Ben Popken on Jalponik.com, a popular online automotive blog. This is a case where a dealership clearly misunderstood the power of the internet and how educated consumers are in the Zero Moment of Truth (remember, Jim Lecinski's book?).

Popken shared in his regular column, called "Stealerships," a story about a dealership that posted a supplemental window sticker on a Hyundai Elantra that included a dealer-installed charge of $1,495 for door edge guards.

Popken researched the door edge guards and found them on eBay for $8. He also did some market research and called Pohanka Hyundai of Marlow Heights, another dealer in the market. Popken asked what Pohanka would charge for these same door edge guards. The answer: $100 installed.

As a result of this one online article, in just 48 hours, 31 negative reviews were posted on Google Places (recently merged with Google+

Local) for the dealership charging $1,495 for the door guards. Google business listings for dealers (including reviews) are displayed tens of thousands of times a month on the first page of search results. This one business directory will amplify the negative press that this dealer just received, every day, and direct in-market shoppers to that dealer's local competitors.

Please keep in mind that this is only one blog post. What happens if this story hits local newspapers, other blogs and automotive forums? The days of internal dealership missteps being disconnected from influencing the next car buyer are over.

The dealer did nothing illegal by increasing the price of the car using the supplemental window sticker, which listed dealer-installed options. What they didn't understand is the power of the internet in regards to pricing. They assumed consumers would not be educated about the cost of door edge guards. Did they forget that consumers comparison shop local dealers all the time?

A unified marketing vision has to ensure that all your marketing and advertising have a consistent message. Your radio, TV, newspaper, billboards, online banners, websites and blogs should all be working together to leverage the power of the internet.

The internet has great potential to build your brand more cost effectively than any other medium. Dealers that have superior customer service can amplify that message using positive customer reviews and video testimonials. The internet forces dealers to take the higher road or accept the consequences. Dealers must avoid falling into the trap of doing what their competition is doing, regardless of the ethical implications.

A case in point is bait and switch advertising. You may know what I'm talking about before I even give an example. Fortunately, the numbers of dealers practicing this tactic are decreasing, but the strategy is to create print advertisements that list a $20,000 vehicle for $12,000 with an asterisk next to the price.

When you read the disclaimer, it states that the price is a combination of the following incentives/rebates:

• Military Rebate
• First Time Buyer Rebate

- College Graduate Rebate
- Conquest Rebate
- Pink Elephant Owner Rebate
- Dealer Cash
- Delta Airline Employee Rebate
- OEM Rebate
- Webbed Foot Rebate

The odds that any one consumer could qualify for the combined discount is slim; pink elephants are rare these days. This type of advertising ignores the power of the internet and customer reviews.

One dealer that practiced this was the recipient of dozens of scathing reviews on Google. Consumers read and are influenced by reviews. A recent study found that 28 percent of consumers said that reviews changed their decision where to buy a car.

Ask yourself this question after reading the review below. Would you buy a car from this dealer after reading the Google review shown below, even if you were about to drive over to the dealership for a scheduled appointment?

"I can't stress enough how you should avoid this place. Unless you want to be fooled, bullied around from salesperson to sales manager, only to find out that the price they advertise on the on the internet is completely phony, as it considers every possible discount, for which you will never qualify. Or do you think you can be in the armed forces, working for UPS and Delta Airlines, have a current car lease, all at the same time??? So the price went from $34K advertised on their own website to a MSRP of $40.5K, that would come down to a mere $37.5 with the discounts I 'qualified' for... A complete SCAM, with shady and rude people, that forced me get up and say I was leaving, only to hear, 'Where are you going?' and I said 'Home!' and heard back: 'That is some way of negotiating'... They even asked me, since I am a salesman myself, if I told my customers 'all the truth' when advertising... I said 'this is not advertising. This is misleading your consumers!!' Their answer: 'Haven't you heard of creative advertising' So if you go there... Good luck.'

The internet can be a dealer's friend or foe. Dealers must put all their business processes through a pink slime filter. Anything they would not want shared on ABC News is best resolved now before the reality of internet transparency takes hold and brings down their business in the local community.

CHAPTER 6

Did You Hire Them Dead or Kill Them After You Got Them?

By Craig Lockerd

The way dealerships make the decision to bring on more salespeople and how they replace underperforming salespeople has always baffled me. I've seen countless formulas, statistical data and seasonal hiring decisions, but very few of these models make any sense. I've even had managers tell me they need four salespeople, and when I asked why four, they respond by saying, "That's how many desks we have open!"

LAW OF DIMINISHING RETURN

The Law of Diminishing Returns in terms of hiring employees at a dealership can be simplified into three stages:

- *Stage one* is the addition of more salespeople, which allows for specialization of job responsibilities and increased production efficiency. The result is a larger output return for each additional unit of input.

- *Stage two* is where inputs equal outputs. Each new salesperson added will continue to increase production but only at the same rate as the increased input of labor.

- *Stage three* is when additional salespeople will start to decrease production efficiency because the work environment is fixed in the short-run. This results in returns that are much less than the labor input.

Do dealers have any idea where that third stage is for their dealership? The ideal outcome at the dealership should be to have as many people as possible buy the dealer's products and services at the highest possible profit margins and deliver 100 percent customer satisfaction. Dealers can't achieve that outcome unless they've maximized the quantity of quality, properly recruited, screened, interviewed and trained salespeople.

I can hear a dealer or general manager object and say, "I don't want to flood my floor." That's admiral, and I applaud their moral judgment in trying to make sure their salespeople all make a good living. However, how many times has a dealer invested in having a special sale, and they look around on the day of the event and notice that several of their salespeople decided to come in late. How many dealers have invested millions into their store and sales staff just to see them leave for a hot, new store that opened up down the road?

Take a minute to write down how many hours a salesperson is currently scheduled to be at the dealership. Would an additional shift or shifts allow them to work fewer hours and be more effective? Would working fewer hours allow sales professionals to have a better quality of life, if that is what would make them more loyal to the store?

Would a more robust staff scheduling model also help dealers deal with talented sales professionals at the dealership who have occasional "manageritis"; employees who have threatened to leave if they don't receive a promotion?

IS MORE BETTER?

How much time do salespeople have to create more business when they're at the dealership bell to bell? Did the dealership sell more cars when it had more sales staff?

Some rural dealers are selling 5 to 10 times more cars than dealers in major metro areas. While there are several factors involved in this, the definitive answer is this: Dealers need better recruited and trained salespeople. I want to share my insights on how dealers can achieve world-class results through better recruiting and training.

Judy B. Margolis, writes: "Employees who grow too comfortable and complacent lose their edge. The more they know, or think they know, about how their particular slice of the business world works, the less likely they are to challenge their old tried-and-true methodologies and to innovate. The same holds true for companies that fail to embrace change, and instead have it foisted upon them, often when it is too late.

HOW TO RECRUIT

When a GM/GSM decides it's time to hire salespeople, they may post a job opening in the newspaper, Craigslist, or CareerBuilder, or post something on an industry job board and expect candidates to start rolling in immediately. It's also likely that they may even suggest that their existing salespeople go to the mall and look for good candidates. This rarely, if *ever*, yields a promising candidate.

So the classified ad is placed and what happens?

- Candidates will call but when transferred, they go to a manager's voice mail. These calls may or may not get returned.

- Candidates walk in, but the manager is busy, so they are told to wait......and wait......and wait....and then....the candidate leaves.

- Candidates walk in and leave a resume. They never get called back because the resume was buried or there was no procedure where resumes should be placed.

Does this recruiting process sound familiar? Dealers are missing great candidates. This practice paints a very poor picture of the automotive retail industry.

WHAT HASN'T CHANGED IN 50 YEARS

Everything changes constantly and rapidly except one thing—what people want. This survey came out in 1946 in "Foreman Facts," from the Labor Relations Institute of New York, and was produced again in 1949 by Lawrence Lindahl in *Personnel* magazine. Here's what employees say they want, starting with what's most important to them:

1. Full appreciation for work done

2. Feeling "in" on things

3. Sympathetic help on personal problems

4. Job security

5. Good wages

6. Interesting work

7. Promotion/growth opportunities

8. Personal loyalty to workers

9. Good working conditions

10. Tactful discipline

Now take a look at what managers think employees want, starting with what they *think* is most important:

1. Good wages

2. Job security

3. Promotion/growth opportunities

4. Good working conditions

5. Interesting work

6. Personal loyalty to workers

7. Tactful discipline

8. Full appreciation for work done

9. Sympathetic help with personal problems

10. Feeling "in" on things

Dealers need to structure their help wanted ads based on what the employee wants to achieve. There are so many success stories at car dealerships, like the former forklift operator I knew who was able to buy his family a beautiful new home because of the training and mentoring the dealership provided.

Top commissions don't necessarily translate into something positive to the candidate reading a job posting. Candidates don't understand what "tons of inventory to sell" means; they might think that the dealership is having trouble selling cars! Employment ads must have strong "hooks," and I will share some winning templates with readers.

THE INTERVIEW

When the candidate arrives at the dealership, what does the interview process look like?

- "So what makes you think you can sell cars?"
- "Why did you leave your last job?"
- "Can you handle 60-hour workweeks?"
- "How do you feel about working with a bunch of men hitting on you everyday?"
- "Sell me this pen."

Do these questions sound familiar? Have they ever worked? My guess is, not often. Dealers need to rethink their interview process.

Visit www.UnfairAdvantageBooks.com for a list of proven ad templates and interview questions that will give you an Unfair Advantage.

SCREENING

Use a predictive index or screening tool in addition to your interview process: Wunderlick, D.I.S.C, AVA, or The Car Sales Simulator by Hire the Winners.

The dealership screening processes, personal investigations, drug testing, DMV and background checks must be done fast! Top talent may not wait two weeks for the results; dealers need to tailor their process to the job seeker, not the other way around.

TRAINING

Dealers must invest in a strong training program, yet many have reduced training investments from their budget while others make excuses:

Excuse: What if I train my salespeople, and they leave?

Response: What if you don't and they stay?

Dealers will train new candidates either in-house or in conjunction with an outside training program. The outsourced training can be online courses or live workshops. Once the training is completed, dealers must consider the processes they have in place to retain and inspect their training investment.

After a limited training period, it's common for a new employee to be placed on the floor to take "ups." The first customer arrives and the new salesperson greets them just the way he/she was trained to do. The customer grabs a brochure and leaves without ever speaking with a manager.

The manager calls the new salesperson over for a recap, and the employee responds with an excuse, which can be:

- Oh, they were just looking.
- Kicking tires on their lunch hour,
- His wife was next door shopping and he was killing time.
- They were asking for directions.
- Their car was getting an oil change.

Since this was the 15th customer who visited the showroom today without one sale, the manager informs the new salesperson (in your best Alex Baldwin voice from "Glengarry Glen Ross") "Coffee is for Closers, Kid." The new employee cowers back into his office.

At the end of the day, the manager remembers yelling at the "Green Pea." The manager sits down with the new hire and informs them that he/she will be trailing "Five Car Fred" the rest of the week.

Fast-forward three weeks, and one of two things have happened:

- The new hire has settled in nicely due to the training of Five Car Fred and has quickly become Four Car Frank.
- You look around and the new hire has blown out and gone on to become the CEO of Burger Doodle down the street.

DID YOU HIRE THEM DEAD OR KILL THEM AFTER YOU GOT THEM?

This type of typical outcome can stop if a dealer is willing to step back and rethink their training program at the dealership. Failed recruitment and training processes can be easily fixed. Dealers must take an honest look at their processes and ask if they are really working to produce the desired outcome they want.

WHAT ARE WE SELLING?

In the book *The One Minute Salesperson*, author Spencer Johnson, M.D. says: "People don't buy our products, services or ideas; they buy how they imagine using them will make them feel!"

What logical sense does it make for any consumer to buy a vehicle that will be worth thousands less than they paid as soon as they drive off the dealership lot? Their purchase has an emotional aspect that cannot be ignored.

Dealership training must focus on the emotions and feelings of in-market car shoppers. Two basics things motivate humans: avoiding pain and seeking pleasure. Dealers should train their staff to direct conversations with their clients toward those feelings that will give them the pleasure they are seeking,

RETHINKING TRAINING FREQUENCY

Car dealers need to train their sales staff every day! They may think that they don't have the material for daily training, but they are wrong. A dealer's sales staff can easily conduct their own training meetings daily. The GM/GSM should be the training facilitator and the person who holds their team accountable, not the content provider.

The sales meeting facilitator can walk into a meeting with a portable white board in hand. The facilitator starts by asking the sales team what is a situation that someone is having trouble overcoming. They write it on the board. Then they go around the room and ask if anyone else is having the same problem; heads will nod affirmatively.

The facilitator then asks who has a solution that they would like to share. Veteran salespeople love to give green peas and those that are struggling their opinion.

In this scenario, someone else will chime in and the salespeople are engaged. The sales team actually starts training each other, and the facilitator keeps the discussion going. There is never a lack of material and conversation when this strategy is used.

KEEPING THE TEAM MOTIVATED

I don't care how much dealers train their sales team, spiff them, yell at them, threaten them or beg them. Salespeople will not be motivated until dealers understand what their real "why" is. Their "why" that is a "must," instead of a "should."

Sales managers need to take five minutes at the start of each month to sit with each salesperson and see what it is they absolutely "must" have this month or quarter or year. I'm not talking about number of units sold or money made. I'm talking about their "why."

Managers should encourage sales professionals to express what it is they really want, which will become their "why." The manager should write down their "why." Let's say one employee's "why" is to get a new home. The manager then investigates why is the new home a "must," rather than a "should." In this case, the salesperson just had another child and needs more room.

Too often, we all say, "I should do this" or "I should do that," and pretty soon we end up should-ing all over ourselves. Have you ever found yourself under a big pile of should? I know I have.

Once the manager has the salesperson's "why" and "must," they need to obtain the "feeling."

Remember this quote from earlier: "People don't buy our products, services or ideas; they buy how they imagine using them will make them feel?" The salesperson's "why" is a feeling. The sales manager must ask the salesperson how it will make them "feel" to get their family moved into a bigger home.

The salesperson will answer, and the sales manager should write down how they'll measure the employee's progress, because you can't manage that which you can't measure. Their answer might be to create a separate "new home account." Finally, the sales manager should ask the salesperson to write down what results they're not getting that they need in order to accomplish their "why."

Managers who follow this recommended process should give a copy of the discussion to the employee and keep a copy at their desk. The next time a salesperson says their clients won't follow the dealership's proven processes, the sales manager can pull out that folder and open it to their "why."

The manager will remind the salesperson of the commitments they made to themselves and will see to it that the salesperson follows the processes correctly every time. After a while, all the manger will need to do is reach toward the drawer that file is in, and the employee will get back on track.

TAPPING INTO THE MARKETPLACE

I often hear dealers proclaim that it's very difficult to find good salespeople for their dealership. I want to challenge that thinking, especially at a time when we have record unemployment.

Could it be that the benefits of working at a dealership are cloudy at best? Dealers cannot afford to ignore the tried-and-true wisdom of Fortune 500 companies and other dealers that publish best practices for attracting, training and retaining employees.

Talented superstars are in every local market looking for a new start a fresh career. Dealerships offer an outstanding career opportunity compared to other businesses in the local market. Dealers who want an Unfair Advantage must revise their HR practices and invest in training and retention.

About Craig

Craig has been in the auto industry for more than 38 years, holding literally every position in a dealership. He became a turnaround consultant in the late '80s and started AutoMax Recruiting and Training more than 13 years ago, because there was an overwhelming need for fresh blood in the auto industry. Craig has personally trained and developed thousands of salespeople and managers while AutoMax Recruiting and Training has conducted more 11,000 recruiting campaigns and has trained over 100,000 people into the auto industry, from "Porters to Presidents." When it comes to cutting-edge recruitment of top talent for the auto industry and how to develop and retain that talent, Craig and his team from AutoMax are the industry leaders!

A highly sought-after speaker, Craig has spoken at numerous 20 Groups, dealerships and industry conferences. Currently, Craig is working on his first book.

While Craig has had much success in his life, he prefers to be defined by his love for the church and his family.

CHAPTER 7

No Gifts, Gimmicks or Gizmos! How to Get Real Buyers Onto Your Lot Using Direct Mail

By Troy Spring

Let's face it, most managers and dealers have a love-hate relationship with direct mail, but they love that it's the most direct results-oriented advertising they use. Bottom line, when they need to move the needle fast it produces the big results they need when done right. They hate the flops, because they do, in fact, happen, and when they do, it hurts like crazy because they counted on their number-one source to produce and it let them down. We have all been in the meeting on the eighth of the month, when the start to the month is horrendous, and said these words (or heard them): "We need to do a mailer!" Then you inevitably hear this statement from someone in the room: "No way, last mailer we lost our tail." The issue is that most direct mail companies are run by people who never sold a car before. There is a certain disconnect between the direct marketing company and what the GSM and salespeople want.

I call this disconnect the "Triangle of Love and Hate." Here is a short story I think you will connect with:

"The Triangle of Love and Hate."

Main characters:

- The Check Writer
- The GSM
- The Direct Mail Guy

There are three people in this triangle, the owner or GM (we will call him the check writer), the GSM and the direct mail guy. The check writer has a nice office that overlooks the lot, and he wants to see cars driving on the lot. The GSM wants to work deals, sell cars, and not get yelled at by the check writer, and the direct mail guy wants to collect his "check" from the check writer and give him the traffic on the lot that he was paid for. The issue is this: One day long, long ago the direct mail guy ran out of ideas to put people on the lot and came up with this brilliant idea to save his ass. He told the check writer they would have loads of people on the lot because he was going to give away a free gift just for coming in. Maybe it would be gold coins, a gift card to Wal-Mart, a three-day cruise voucher with insane port fees. Wait, maybe a socket wrench set, or a turkey for Thanksgiving, maybe an umbrella—yeah, and umbrella would awesome. You get the idea. The good news for the direct mail guy is that the check writer likes being right, so when 200 people showed up to get the umbrella they both sat in the check writer's office in utter awe of how smart they are. Love was created between the check writer and the direct mail guy.

Downstairs there was hate brewing. The GSM who had to do all the work and try and manage 200 people driving on his lot and disrupting normal business was pulling his hair out. He had his skilled and trained salespeople coming to him left and right complaining the people they just "upped" only wanted the free umbrella, and that was the sixth one in a row. Right after that, the check writer called a meeting with all managers to ask them why they could not close a barn door if it had a stiff wind behind it. "Seventy-four ups, one deal. It's a deal we had hanging anyways, and it's already 2 pm," he shouted. "I spent $17,000 on this mailer, and it has to work, so what are we doing wrong?"

Not one manager dared to say what they were really thinking because they like paying their mortgages too much, but if they did, they would say something like this: "I am not going to go T.O. on every blue-haired old lady who wants an umbrella. It's disrupting our normal business, and there's a chance we might sell less cars today because we are not in our element. As a matter of fact, I think we are great at not pre-judging customers and working them hard, but when nine people in a row want the stinking umbrella, it is hard for the best of us not to get negative and assume the at the tenth is any different. So I am sure we are treating our real buyers like gifties and losing a few deals."

But like I said, that was just a dream because he won't say that. He will say the salesmen are not working hard enough. The same sales guys who make you profitable day in and day out all of a sudden hit the stupid button, and they need to be trained better. "My fault boss, sorry we are on it." The GSM does not want to blame the direct mail guy; after all, they had 74 people in so far, 72 of which wanted to waste his time.... but 74 all the same.

An hour later the direct mail guy calls the check writer from somewhere off-site, maybe on a boat somewhere or in a cubicle wearing his headset, and asks: "How is it going buddy; I see we got 100 people to the website?" (All there to see if they won a million dollars." The check writer responds, "Well, you did your job: We have 74 people so far but off to a slow start. I just had a meeting with the guys to see what the heck is going on down there?" The moral of the story is that the check writer allows the direct mail guy to hide behind "crap" traffic and place all the accountability on the wrong guy—his GSM. I've seen him even fire good managers over poor performance of not turning the blue-haired-umbrella guests in to deals. The triangle of love and hate is complete. The only two in love are the direct mail guy and the check writer. The problem really starts with the fact that the person designing the mailer has never taken an up, worked a deal or closed one. It is impossible for him to understand the culture of a showroom floor or the disruption it forces.

Imagine the Unfair Advantage you would have as a dealer doing direct mail if you knew that the "guy" you are buying from has, in fact, closed more than 10,000 deals himself, worked the floor for more than 500 mailer events, and actually takes time away from the job of selling mail to enter his "think tank" and develop from scratch new events and themes that are strong enough to drive real buyers to the lot. Remember at the beginning of this chapter I stated that one day, the direct mail guy gave in and had no more ideas on how to drive buyers, so he satisfied the check writer with "people." Well, the Unfair Advantage you could have is if you identify those perpetrators that disguise themselves as car guys and pawn off gift-seeking traffic as ups. Once you identify them and understand their system is a broken one and that delivery direct to the mailbox with a hard-hitting message about buying cars is still the best ROI available today, you will be on your way to dominating your market with direct mail again.

The idea is as hard as finding a needle in a haystack. Think of it this way: The next time you do a mailer think of the buyers who show up as needles and the gift seekers as hay. Trying to find a buyer in the midst of 200 gift seekers wasting your time is as hard as finding a needle in a haystack. It can be done, but it requires focus and determination for hours and hours. Can you see the analogy? Imagine now that only needles showed up for the big sale. Sure you would lose the hype and excitement of people running all over the place. We all know the advantage of props, heck everyone of us has let some folks sit for an extra 10 minutes in the showroom to make it look busy. So one day pondering all this, I asked myself a crazy question: What if I could bring enough needles to make the showroom look busy?

When I set out to do this, many people thought I was crazy. Most of them were other direct mail friends of mine, in particular many of them making a living in the super sale business. They certainly did not want to think or believe that it could be done any other way than what was making them millions.

True Story:

One day I sat in my office and closed the door. I got out a blank sheet of paper and started from scratch. I took out all the things I did not like from the GSM's perspective. (As you now know, I feel he is the key to this mail stuff working.) I set out to do the impossible. I felt that the three people you could target with a mailer—in order of how easy it is to get them in the door—are: 1) the giftie, 2) the subprime candidate, and 3) the hardest was a real buyer, who is able to buy a car and in the market to buy one. I set out to design a mailer to target the hardest of the three to get in the door—a real, pure buyer interested in buying a car. I thought if I can bring enough of them in, I could create a buyers' frenzy but with all buyers, not props, and the result would be a huge closing ratio. I was right—when you have a showroom full of people who want to buy cars, something magical happens.

So here are a few things to consider when buying direct mail to give you the Unfair Advantage:

1. *Never ask the response rate again; ask for delivery ratio.* It is a stupid question to ask a guy who knows the higher he makes it, the more you will listen to him: 2 percent, 3 percent, 4 percent ... what do you want to hear?

   At Dealer World, I tell clients when they ask that it's the worst in the industry. After a blank stare for a few seconds and trying not to get kicked out, I say, "Would you like to know why I think you should do business with us? I just told you I do not target the two easiest people in the world to bring in to the store: the gift seeker and the credit-challenged customer—how could I possibly have a high or highest response rate?" Now that the stage is set so I can explain that while high-response companies can say they had 500 people in over five days, how many of them said they delivered 200 to 300 cars? Normally that type of traffic is tied to a delivery ratio of maybe 5 to 8 percent, or 25 to 40 cars. I can say with all sorts of conviction that you do not need 500 people to sell 40 cars.

2. *Ask yourself, if you could bring in 80 to 300 people who want to buy cars, would it be better than 500 to 800 people who do not want to buy cars?* Would you rather have salespeople closing at 25 to 40 percent, or 5 to 8 percent?

3. *When looking at mailers, ask yourself what is the hook that makes them want to buy a car or know that we are serious about selling cars?* Are you doing the "Summer Sizzler Sales Event?" What the heck does that mean? Are you giving out turkeys because it is Thanksgiving? How does that sell cars?

   Pick your company based on what they do differently to bring you buyers and the originality of the program they have. If they have a different twist and a strong idea, give them some time and listen. They probably at least have some thought behind what they are doing and a strong belief system.

4. ***Smaller companies that do not own a printer can be your best value.*** They have no machines to pay for, no huge buildings, and infrastructure to pay for. Pricing from them can get you a similar product for far less money if shopped right. You need great ideas first and foremost. Proof that direct mail is still the best and fastest most focused ROI. Ask any super sale company that depends on making a living every week on the road away from their family what they use to drive traffic. Not one person who relies on big traffic and profits week in, week out depends on anything else except direct mail. The proof is in the profits.

Bottom line: In order to claim the Unfair Advantage in direct mail, do not be afraid of a strong message that says you are selling cars! Do lots of it with a reputable company and trust that you are branding yourself to the masses who will receive it as well as reaping the rewards of the best direct and fasted ROI still available in today's market.

About Troy

Troy "Turbo" Spring, President of Dealer World, is best known for *breaking records and innovations in the direct mail business*. His no gift, no gimmick "Hyper Mail" hits like OverstockedCarLots.com, iWantANewCar.TV, and HalfPricedCars.com have done just that over and over again. While most direct mail companies hide behind the traffic of gifts, Troy's passion for providing value led him to develop themes and events that held Dealer World accountable to traffic that consist of only buyers. He has been quoted as saying, "No turkeys, no basketballs, no keys, no socket wrench sets, and no Wal-Mart gift cards. My job is to put people on your lot who want to buy cars. If I cannot do that, than you do not need me."

With more than 20 years in direct mail and consulting, he has performed more than 650 direct mail events, personally ran over 500 of them (himself, no teams) from start to finish and closed more than 10,000 car deals personally. Now consulting for dealers and other outside businesses using the same go-big-or-go-home principles, he has been able to increase profits dramatically at every business he has "touched." For this reason, along with his energy and focus, he was nicknamed "Turbo" by his friends and co-workers. He is now completing his first book "Turbo Charge Your Life," explaining his systems and beliefs on what earned him that nickname. With his extensive direct mail and radio experience, he speaks on how traditional media is still viable and provides the best ROI. He can and will show you how to maximize your returns with it and how he used his formula to *break records* at every store he ran or consulted for in the past 20 years.

Should you have any comments or questions, feel free to reach out to Troy Spring at troyspring@mac.com.

CHAPTER 8

Same Is Lame: How to Stand Out and Sell More Without Spending More

By Jimmy Vee and Travis Miller

Most people hate car dealers. That hate is based on a stereotype—and it's unfair.

Today, unfortunately, most car dealers are actually helping this stereotype live on and flourish. Not because they treat their customers badly. In fact, you probably treat your customers very well. The stereotype lives on because dealers permit consumers to group all dealerships into the same category; most dealerships look, act, sound and feel the same. So they must all be the same, right?

Of course, that's an assumption that may or may not be true. Are you really the same? Or is there a good reason for customers to choose you over other dealerships in your area? There should be. That's the first big lesson in this chapter. Highlight it.

WHAT MAKES YOUR STORE SPECIAL?

Are you thinking about low price, good location, great service, quality vehicles? So is *everybody* else! There's never been a car dealer who promised high prices, bad location, terrible service and junk cars.

Your store can't be special by being the same, looking the same and saying the same things. Quite specifically, in business today, *same is lame*. And if you look up "lame" in the dictionary, you'll find that it means "pathetically lacking in force or effectiveness." You should highlight that, too.

Given the nasty stereotype that dealers face, seeming the same as all other dealerships is a pretty poor strategy. If your store is like all the others, well, people will want to hate you. That can be a drag on sales.

Understandably, there's tremendous pressure these days from various powers for all dealerships to look the same. It's homogenization and commoditization at work, and it's a negative force that hurts dealers. You must do everything in your power to buck the trend...to look different, think different and actually be different than other dealerships.

If your store doesn't fit the stereotype, why should you run the risk of being victimized by prejudice? The good news is you can fight back—with a vengeance!

Following are strategies you can use to make a bold and clear statement that you are not that stereotypical car dealer. By doing so, you'll find it easier and more efficient to attract customers, make sales, and increase gross and net profit. You'll stand out and sell more without spending more money in the process.

STOP WAITING, START ATTRACTING

Selling cars today is a lot like fishing. The ocean is the internet. The fish are the customers. The bait is cars and prices.

The common belief is that today's customers are so enlightened, so empowered and so knowledgeable, that the only thing left to do is to wait for customers to decide it's the right time to buy, wait for them to decide on the vehicle they want, and wait for them to finish their research and find the lowest price. Hopefully, when that time comes, you'll have the car. Hopefully, you have the lowest price. Hopefully, they'll contact you.

But waiting is not a success strategy. In fact, if you really want an Unfair Advantage, you should decide to *hate the wait*. Highlight that.

Most dealers are perfectly capable of greatly accelerating the process. Most stores are ready to begin enjoying a steady stream of qualified buyers who seek them out specifically, who are excited to do business with them and only them.

But here's the scary reality: Most never will. They will continue to wait and make excuses and justifications for why a competitor always seems to have more market share and make more money while they are struggling just to stay afloat and working way too hard in the process.

These dealers aren't broken. There is a fix. The problem is not with them. They just don't know how and why people are attracted to a particular dealership. They don't realize that all the common, customary and ordinary things they're doing (like advertising prices and vehicles) are only making them less attractive and more of a commodity…only perpetuating the negative stereotype.

Attraction isn't a choice made by customers. It's a force. The customer doesn't make a conscious choice between your store and another dealership. They are attracted, pulled to you, as if by a powerful, natural force. They can't escape it.

Here's how it works: Everyone wants to make good decisions in their lives. The problem is that good decision-making requires searching, information gathering, comparison and analysis. That's all frustrating and time consuming. Frankly, most people just aren't well enough equipped to manage the process. Not to mention, it really seems like a lot of work, and most people don't want to work too hard.

This is one of the major reasons customer attraction is possible. Most people need help and want help streamlining the decision-making process. They're terrified of making the wrong decision. They are looking for a shortcut and are willing to pay for it. They're looking for a trusted advisor. If you position your dealership as a source of help, guidance and security, you'll find that people flock to your store rather than go it alone in the wild world.

Beyond that, people are desperately seeking a buying preference. That is, a reason to choose one dealership over another. Since most dealerships all look the same, it's very difficult for customers to develop their own buying preference. There's a gaping hole waiting for a dealer to fill in most markets by positioning their store as the "obvious choice," instead of "just another car dealership with cars and prices."

Finally, people can be motivated to "buy now and buy here" rather than "buy later and buy somewhere else." Usually, all it takes is an irresistible offer—a compelling reason to buy now—and it really should be something other than low price, because low price is a constant in the car business today.

By providing information, being an expert resource, making irresistible offers and creating a buying preference you can help customers make the good decisions they are seeking and help them do it in record time. They'll feel good about it and you'll get a customer for life. This is attraction in action.

We believe that most dealers have the natural ability to promote their dealerships in a way that makes them attract, pull and gravitate prospects and customers, but they've just never cultivated that natural ability.

Instead, pop culture, parents, politicians, past experiences, traditional education, industry best practices and all kinds of other things have hidden and stunted the development of this talent.

Learning how to attract customers instead of waiting for them is the only way to grow and prosper in the car business today. There are many benefits given to those who tap into their natural ability to do this. For instance, your business and your life become ESP—Enjoyable, Simple & Prosperous, and you truly develop an Unfair Advantage.

STOP SELLING CARS, START SELLING SOLUTIONS

Take a moment and let that sink in. Stop selling cars and start selling solutions. Solutions are what people seek every day. Our lives are hectic. We have no time. We're stressed. We're frustrated. We've got problems. Can you identify with all that?

People are looking for solutions to those problems, to those stresses and frustrations, to the things that are wasting their time. They're looking for a solution to make them feel better, to make their pain go away. When you start selling that, when your marketing is about that, not prices and vehicles, you'll start seeing a lot more traffic!

This is the key to selling a lot more cars and earning a lot more profit and making your customers a lot happier and more willing to refer and come back for service.

Now you can radically change the type of customer and process by which you sell cars, the process by which you attract customers by increasing your value proposition, by focusing on being a solutions provider.

Often, a potential car buyer wants to upgrade their vehicle but has challenges and obstacles in their way that they don't know how to remove. Fear, misinformation and lack of knowledge are holding them back. But you have the power to help! You have the solutions to their problems!

In fact, there are more people with problems who don't intend to buy a car right now than there are people without problems who do intend to buy a car. The biggest opportunity in the car business today is to stop competing with all the other dealerships over price, and start harvesting the massive gains in traffic and sales that come from speaking to the mass market about the problems people all have in common. When you offer to help fix those problems, the customers come rushing in the door and price concerns go flying out the window.

STOP COMPETING ON PRICE, START WINNING ON VALUE

We aren't going to say that price isn't important to customers, because clearly it is. We've all experienced price sensitivity from customers, these days perhaps even more than in the past. But low price is far less valuable than solutions.

When you think about it, there is a lot of talk about value, and most people assume that means lowering prices. The interesting thing about value is that it is as valuable as it is. This means the less valuable something is, the lower the price is, and the more valuable it is, the higher the price is.

Solutions rank much higher in people's minds in value than price alone does. Anybody can sell something for the lowest price. No skill required. It's not so common to find someone who really cares, who will really help and who really adds value.

Customers only turn to price when there are no other factors to consider and when there's really nothing else to choose by. So if you can solve a customer's problem, that has much greater value and they're willing to pay more.

Sadly, price-oriented marketing has become the standard among dealerships today. Most dealers see it as a necessary evil that can't be avoided. Price seems to be the last remaining competitive edge a dealership can employ. But what happens when even that edge dulls?

It's entirely possible to transfer the emphasis of your marketing and communication from price to value. The secret is blending three critical elements that create customer attraction momentum without the slightest mention of price.

1. *Targeting:* Most dealerships logically target the same type of prospect—in-market shoppers, people who are currently searching for cars online or visiting dealership showrooms. We advocate also targeting out-of-market, non-intenders, people who have no intention of buying a vehicle in the coming days or weeks. They're not shopping online or in showrooms, and they typically don't have a vehicle preference. But there is one striking commonality among these non-intenders: The majority of them say they would prefer to driver a nicer, newer car than they currently drive. But without a specific vehicle preference, they also don't have a price preference or concern. The non-intender market is about 50 times larger than the intender market, and most dealership marketing completely ignores it.

2. *Positioning:* Most dealership marketing effectively positions the dealership as a product-oriented business, with pictures of cars, lists of features and prices. But product-oriented messages will do very little to attract the non-intender. Instead, we advocate positioning the dealer (or another person inside the dealership) and the dealership as solutions-oriented, with a focus on solving problems and offering helpful advice, rather than pushing product. This positioning technique significantly lowers buyer anxiety and resistance and helps hasten the building of trust and rapport.

3. *Offers:* Most dealership marketing features price-related offers such as discounts, low payments, rebates or special incentives. Unfortunately, price-related offers do little in the way of attracting non-intenders. We encourage you to make offers that address and promise to solve the specific problems customers (non-intenders) have. Most of the dealers we've worked with have found that switching from a price-related offer to a solutions-related offer in their current advertising

alone will yield a substantial result. As an added benefit, the same offers that attract non-intenders are also extremely appealing to in market shoppers and have proved to be effective alternatives to price-oriented offers.

Price is not the only competitive advantage available to dealers anymore. As the number of in-market buyers decreases or stays depressed, the number of non-intenders grows or stays high. This approach to marketing and selling vehicles can help you stop fighting with other dealers over the same few customers and create your own crop of dedicated and enthusiastic buyers using your natural customer attraction power.

In closing, we'd like to share with you some excellent advice given by the great Earl Nightingale: "If you want to be successful, look at what everyone else is doing, and do the opposite."

Standing out and selling more without spending more money begins with a commitment to break from the pack and the courage to look, think and be different than the other dealers in your town. You'll enjoy the benefits of a life and business that are ESP—Enjoyable, Simple & Prosperous—and enable your dealership to be firmly separated from the nasty car dealer stereotype that causes so much harm.

To receive a complimentary copy of our book, *The Invasion of the Profit Snatchers*, which explores these topics in much greater detail, visit www.ProfitSnatchersBook.com, and use the coupon code UABOOK.

To learn more about how we can help you rapidly implement these ideas at your store, visit www.RichDealers.com.

About Jimmy and Travis

Jimmy Vee

Travis Miller

Jimmy Vee and Travis Miller are the nation's leading experts on attracting customers, the authors of the bestselling book *Gravitational Marketing: The Science of Attracting Customers*, and the founders of Rich Dealers®.

Called "The Penn & Teller of Automotive Marketing," Jimmy and Travis have been helping auto dealers differentiate themselves, attract customers and increase sales for more than a decade. In 2004, they created Rich Dealers®, an exclusive customer attraction agency for busy dealers who want to stand out and sell more without spending more in advertising. It is *the* place for fun and profit in the car business.

Collectively, their campaigns have resulted in the sale of more than 2 million vehicles. Every month they create record-shattering automotive promotions and bring together some of the brightest and most successful dealers, authors, entrepreneurs and businesspeople to participate in fun and insanely profitable "think-thank," mastermind experiences.

Jimmy and Travis have spoken all over the world about their special brand of customer attraction, known as Gravitational Marketing®, and have been seen in *Entrepreneur* magazine, *Investor's Business Daily*, Ripley's Believe It or Not, *Forbes,* CNBC, Fox Business, *Advertising Age, Direct Marketing News, Businessweek, Brandweek, Used Car News, AutoSuccess, Dealer Marketing Magazine, Auto Remarketing,* and many other publications and media outlets.

Jimmy and Travis believe that life and business should be ESP—Enjoyable, Simple & Prosperous. They help make this a reality through their work at Rich Dealers®, freeing car dealers from tedious tasks that keep them bound to the business, worried about profitability, and unable to live their lives to the fullest.

Jimmy and Travis both reside in Orlando, Florida, each married with two young children.

CHAPTER 9

Mastering the Telephone

By Jerry Thibeau

Your dealership, like many others, spent millions building a brick and mortar facility to provide customers with an excellent shopping experience. However, dealerships typically get more phone inquiries per day than actual visits in person, yet very little emphasis is placed on the value of a customer phoning your dealership. This is a pervasive problem within the automotive industry. Typically the phone experience for today's customer does not provide the same quality of experience they receive by visiting the dealership. From fixed to variable operations, customers receive less than marginal experiences. Therefore, what they hear or don't hear on the phone creates a perception of your dealership that a state-of-the-art facility cannot change.

It's time to take your business to the next level. In this chapter, we will examine every facet of just how to provide customers with a world-class phone experience.

When a customer calls your dealership, are they greeted by an automated attendant or a live person? There is no better start to a phone call than hearing a real person on the other end of the phone. An automated phone system may be needed to handle large call volumes. However, a key issue with automated systems is that callers are often routed to voicemail or left on perpetual hold. On average, 26 percent of all customers never reach the intended department or person, and if they do get voicemail, a message is left only 50 percent of the time.

Key points to consider when using an automated phone system:

- The prompt command should start with: "Thank you for calling ABC Motors, at any point should you require an operator, please press 0 for assistance. For service, press 1, for sales..."

- Service is the largest percentage of calls to your dealership and should be a prompt one, followed by sales and parts.

- Routinely check your phone system to make sure all prompts are working properly.

- Spot check your departments to see how quickly calls are answered and returned.

- What happens when a person or department fails to answer? Does the phone ring back to the automated attendant, or does it go to voicemail? In my view, neither is acceptable. The call should be routed to a live operator.

- Use an outside service to leave voicemails to determine how long it takes for your employees to return a call. The longer it takes, the less likely you are to earn a customer's business.

When done right, a live operator answering the phone is the best solution and having the right person in this position is essential. As the Director of First Impressions, your operator sets the tone for the entire dealership. Many dealerships fail to find the right person to fill this position. My advice: Interview, interview, and interview more to find that right personality to fill this key role. If you have to pay a little more to find the right person, then do it. Dealerships spend hundreds of advertising dollars to get the phone to ring, so why not pay a few more dollars an hour to provide a better experience for your customers? Dealerships cannot afford to not get this right when hiring an operator.

Key points to consider when having an operator handle calls.

- The operator needs to understand that it may be the hundredth call he/she has taken, but for the person calling it is probably their first. A customer is your most valued possession.

- Operators should deliver a clear and well-prepared greeting such as: "Thank you for calling ABC motors, how may I direct your call?" Inserting their name in the greeting is preferred, but not required. They may also deliver a dealership value proposition message by inserting something like "home of the lifetime warranty" or any other value proposition that sets your dealership apart from the competition. Avoid long-winded messages.

- When transferring a customer, always inform the customer of your intentions, such as: "One moment please while I transfer your call to service."

- If your phone system does not have the ability to monitor what's happening with a caller, then I strongly suggest having the operator keep the caller on hold while paging the appropriate department. Never let go of a customer until you know they are being helped.

- Transferring a customer to voicemail should be a last resort since only 50 percent of customers actually leave a message. Have your operator take a written message. "I am going to have (department or person) call you back. Should they call you at home or work? And that number is? How do I spell your last name correctly? And your first name is?" If that person is unavailable, then have someone else return the customer's call.

Have you ever called home and gotten your spouse on the phone, and within a few seconds knew exactly what type of mood he or she was in? Customers immediately get a feel for your mood based on how you answer the phone. Often we rush through greetings leaving the customer thinking that we don't have time for them and are in a hurry to get them off the phone. When the operator transfers the caller to the appropriate person or department, each employee in your dealership should understand the importance of a proper phone greeting.

Tips for delivering a great initial greeting:

- Answer the phone with an upbeat tone and message.

- Smile, this actually helps deliver a positive vibe.

- Use your first name only as this is easier for the customer to remember. There will be plenty of time later in the call to provide your last name.

- Be prepared! Have a pen and paper handy for taking notes. Know your current advertisements.

- Take it slowly and never rush through your greeting.

Once a proper greeting is delivered, it is time to strive for the ultimate goal: the appointment. A "sale" is not the goal of a phone call because, although it can be made in certain cases with parts and showroom sales, those who try to sell over the phone generally experience a lower closing ratio and often make less profit.

To obtain an appointment, it is always best to take the time to uncover your customers' needs by asking qualifying questions. Qualifying allows you to build rapport with your customer while assessing their needs. Proper qualifying motivates the customer to want to do business with you. More important, you are asking questions that give you control of the call.

Some tips for investigating customers' needs:

SALES

- Ask three to five good closed-ended questions, such as: "Are you looking for a new vehicle or pre-owned? Do you want a five speed or are you looking for an automatic? Would you prefer a lighter or darker shade?"

- Since 70 percent of all calls originate on a specific vehicle, build confidence in the customer's choice. On specific vehicle calls, deliver the following message: "That's a really nice vehicle, and we've had a few calls on that one recently." This tells the customer what they want to hear and confirms the vehicle is a nice choice. You will also find it easier to set an appointment sooner than later since others are considering the same vehicle. Don't forget to find out about other vehicles the customer is considering because many will purchase a different vehicle from the one about which they initially inquired.

SERVICE

- Ask questions about the customer's vehicle as though you were a doctor investigating an illness. And like a doctor, do not prescribe a solution until you see the patient.

- When customers explain their issues, try to show some empathy and put yourself in their shoes. A little compassion goes a long way toward earning customer trust. For example, "I am sorry to hear your radiator experienced a leak. I had that happen to me once and it was not fun, so I can understand your frustration."

PARTS

- Ask questions about the vehicle to determine the proper part(s) needed. Compliment the customer on their vehicle of choice, such as: "That's a nice vehicle, have you had it since day one?" This is a great opportunity to build rapport.

- Ask the customer if they plan to install the part themselves or have the work done in the service department. Many people will call to ask for a price, and once it is given, the call ends with nothing more accomplished.

At some point during the call, obtain the customer's name and contact information. Many fail at this technique for the simple reason that they do not provide the customer with a good reason to provide this information. Many also fail because of the weak manner in which they ask.

Here are some techniques to use when obtaining contact information:

SALES

- "So I don't waste your time, let me check to see if that vehicle is available and if we have any others. Are you calling from home or work...and that number is? How do I spell your last name and your first name?"

SERVICE AND PARTS

- "So I can look your vehicle up in our system, please spell your last name correctly, your first name is, and the telephone number associated with your vehicle is?"

When it comes to an appointment, I am amazed at how few even ask for one, and those who do will generally do so in a weak manner. Asking a question that can easily yield a yes or no answer should be avoided. Using weak words such as maybe, possibly, think, or around will generally result in low appointment percentages. When asking for the appointment, do it with confidence. The greater the confidence, the more likely the customer will follow your lead.

"When would you like to come in, now or later today?" This is a very assumptive question and is the proper way to ask for an appointment. Two choices were given, and the customer is expected to pick one. If we change the question to: "Could you come in today or tomorrow," now we have allowed for a yes or a no response.

Appointment ratios will increase by asking for the appointment properly, but there are times when objections will need to be handled. If properly prepared, objections can be overcome on the telephone. Give your customers value proposition statements. Tell them why they should visit you and your dealership, and what makes you and your dealership better than the competition. After delivering a value proposition statement, ask for the appointment again. If you sense your customer is becoming agitated, settle for a future scheduled action. Avoid letting a customer off the phone without an appointment or a future scheduled action that will be initiated on your part. The future action could be a phone call or an email.

When closing a phone call, make sure your customer is aware of whom they will ask when they arrive by having them write down your name. When writing your name down people are three times more likely to remember your name when they come into the dealership. Always obtain an email address from your customer with the intention of sending an appointment confirmation or to confirm the future action agreed upon.

Confirm directions with callers, even if they tell you they know the location of your dealership. Ask them to tell you the route they will be taking. Surprisingly, many customers pull a number off the web and think they are talking to one dealer when they are really talking to another and then drive to the wrong dealership.

According to the "NADA 2011 Data Report," the average dealership spent 654 advertising dollars per vehicle sold. Here's the big question: How much did you spend properly training your salespeople to handle opportunities that came in via phone? For most dealerships, it's not very much. If you spend the money advertising, be sure your staff is properly trained to handle the opportunities those dollars generate. One without the other is senseless.

With the low-cost call tracking solutions available today, there is no reason why your dealership should not be recording phone conversations. Recorded calls make for great training opportunities. Staff also tend to perform at higher levels when aware they are being monitored.

Phone Ninjas created the industry standard for scoring and coaching phone conversations. The Phone Skills Index (PSI) evaluates a call based on 33 different data points and then provides coaching feedback captured within an audio file. With the thousands of calls we have evaluated and scored, we are able to correlate PSI to specific appointment percentages. Here is a look at different PSI scores and their corresponding appointment percentages.

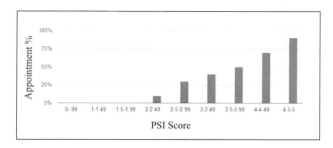

Dealers with PSI scores under 2.0 are not setting appointments. A 50 percent appointment ratio should be the minimum goal for every dealership. In order to achieve this, your dealership must maintain a PSI score of 3.50 to 3.99. Approximately 10 percent of Phone Ninjas' clients maintain an average of 4.00 to 4.49, which yields a 75 percent appointment ratio. Half these dealerships maintain scores above 4.50, with a 90 percent appointment ratio. This is a challenging but not impossible task. It takes a lot of focus, determination and practice to achieve and maintain a high PSI score.

To learn more about PSI scoring and how Phone Ninjas can help your business excel, please email Jerry at jerry@phoneninjas.com or by phone at (877) 475-1830.

About Jerry

Jerry Thibeau is the president and founder of Phone Ninjas, a company focused on helping dealerships improve phone skills. Jerry is a 27-year automotive veteran and has earned the nickname "The Phone Ninja" for his ability to turn even the hardest of phone shoppers into real appointments that show. Having personally listened to and provided coaching feedback on more than 10,000 sales calls, Thibeau is the industry's best and brightest when it comes to evaluating a phone conversation.

In 2011, Jerry logged 142 flights over a span of 40 weeks speaking at dealerships, dealer associations and key industry conferences. Jerry has written countless articles for the industry and is an active blogger on all the popular automotive social media sites.

His company, Phone Ninjas, provides ongoing training to hundreds of dealers across the nation. The Phone Ninjas Phone Skills Index (PSI Score) has become the industry standard for evaluating the effectiveness of a phone conversation. Jerry's success with clients has made Phone Ninjas one of the hottest and fastest-growing companies in the automotive sector. Phone Ninjas was a recent winner of the PCG Spotlight Awards for one of the top five products at NADA 2012.

CHAPTER 10

The Best Tools Are Not Just Found in the Service Bay Toolbox

By Brian Pasch

In 1991, I was moonlighting as an information technology (IT) consultant while working on Wall Street. I remember a conversation I had with the executives of a growing company with more than 40 employees that had a simple Panasonic Key System Unit (KSU). I recommended they invest in an intelligent phone system with voice mail capability. Their reaction still is ingrained in my memory, as almost in perfect unison they objected, "Why would we need voice mail when we have a receptionist?"

Fast forward 20 years, and today's objection is "Why do we need to engage on social media websites when we have a dealership website!" Social media engagement is neither an option nor a wasted investment. Social media is part of the new infrastructure that dealers must invest in to succeed in the same way the dealership wouldn't think of operating without voicemail.

Dealers set on building an Unfair Advantage in their market are learning how to leverage social channels in order to increase brand awareness, drive traffic to their websites, and increase their organic search rankings. Social media is just one tool in the new toolbox that dealers can leverage to service their businesses.

WHY LOCK THE GATE

Those dealers that have decided to limit their employees' access to key social media websites are wasting time, money, and most important, missing a unique branding opportunity. The chance to extend a dealership's brand on social media is well documented, so why do so many dealers think it's unnecessary?

Comically, when dealers block social media sites in the dealership, employees will use their smartphones to leverage these communication channels and bypass the restrictions.

This scenario reminds me of Herb's Liquors in North Plainfield, New Jersey, where I grew up. When I was in high school, the legal drinking age was 18 years old. Can anyone remember being under age and asking an older brother or friend to stop by the package goods store (Herb's) to pick up beer for a high school party? Where there's a will, there's a way!

Savvy sales professionals know they can network effectively using social media. Progressive dealerships are leveraging the delivery process to post photos and videos on Facebook, while others fear this access and lock down these sites.

Change has always scared "corporate" minds and fueled the passion of entrepreneurs. New tools exist for dealers to bring their automotive marketing, sales and retention strategies to the next level. These tools include social media, mobile apps, tablet computing, chat, and advanced CRM software, but is the toolbox locked to their employees? Will training be denied or limited to a select few individuals? I challenge dealers to move from their current place of comfort and embrace the new tools of our industry.

History is filled with examples of executives who predicted the internet was a fad. Today, industry leaders predict that social media is a fad as well. How did that first prediction work out?

It's time for the automotive community to empower their employees to connect with customers however and wherever they choose to engage. The walls of the showroom no longer confine customer communications and access to data, so dealers should seek tools that enhance that new freedom.

Dealers need to stop projecting their personal prejudices on their business models. If a dealer principal decides not to engage on Facebook, that's his choice. Personal choice, however, should not result in a company policy banning Facebook engagement. Preventing employees from accessing the internet during work hours is really not practical.

I've heard dealership managers say that their sales team will spend time surfing porn, checking sports scores, or wasting hours chatting with friends if the internet were open at the dealership. There are ways to block websites with pornography inside the dealership using firewalls. Let's be clear, when I speak of opening access, I'm speaking about the top social media sites that shouldn't be blocked from employees.

> There's a great saying that my friend Rick Ivone repeats often: "What you do in one thing, you do in all things."

If the employees at the dealership choose to waste their time, they're most likely not the right people that will serve the dealership in the long term. In my experience, poor work habits by employees are a reflection of the leadership at the very top of the organization. Painful to hear but so often this is the case.

The commitment and passion of the employees at any company are directly related to the leaders of the company. If dealership employees have no respect for their time and the investment made by their dealer principal, there are bigger problems at play. Internet access is not the biggest one by far!

EDUCATION TRUMPS FEAR

Fear is often the result of misinformation, and no better place can this be seen than in the dealership. Is our industry changing at a very fast pace? Indeed. So what should we do about that? We cannot hide, so we must embrace this change with confidence.

My 15-year-old son Connor is a freshman in high school. We were talking the other day about next year's classes. He said, "I heard sophomore year is really hard." I chuckled inside and asked, "Based on what information?" He shared that math was harder and teachers expected more of the students. His peers who shared a fear-based view of the world intimidated him.

How many of us are guilty of fear-based decisions? Have you told yourself that digital marketing, social media, or CRM systems are too hard for you to understand? Are you using the excuse that you didn't grow up with computers as a way to shirk responsibility for leading your organization?

In regards to education, I encourage all dealers to rethink their investments or avoidance of new technology. Dealers that have a consistent investment in education for their sales, marketing, fixed operations, and back-office personnel will be much better suited to understand, investigate and integrate the new tools of our trade.

By the time this book is published, new tools will be for sale that offer the opportunity for dealers to gain an Unfair Advantage in their market. Unless the dealership's culture can embrace change, the promise of these new tools will be lost. This book is designed to encourage change with winning strategies shared by industry leaders.

Are you ready to lead that change? Open your toolbox and add some new tools and get started! Was your sophomore year really that hard compared to the challenges you've faced in life since you left high school?

CHAPTER 11

Unlocking the Hidden Profits of Reinsurance

By Tim Byrd

It was a Friday in October 1994. I was called into a sales meeting, as I was every Friday, to discuss how we were going to motivate the F&I managers we were tasked to develop. I was an F&I development manager for a company that provided products and training to new car franchise dealerships. My job was to train business managers how to maximize the finance and insurance income in their dealership without sacrificing CSI. I had been with this company for three years and had been an F&I manager (one of the best) for several years prior to being asked to join this company. Every job has its ups and downs, and sales meetings are an opportunity to discuss strategy and motivate your team. This particular day, at this particular meeting, turned out to be a turning point in my life. After a brow beating by our owner, he finished by saying, "If you need us, we will be at the golf course." I decided at that moment that I could do this myself. I did not need to work for someone else! So on October 31, 1994, with a 2 year old and a 2 month old, and my wife, Susan, who was convinced we would soon be living in a cardboard box, I quit my job and stepped out on faith to start Tim Byrd & Associates Inc.

Of course, as all business owners know, there were some very trying moments getting started. Convincing car dealers to put their trust in you is difficult to say the least. Heck, just getting a dealer to give you an audience is a great undertaking. I can remember being very discouraged. It was right before Christmas and I had yet to have one dealer put their trust in me. I was thumbing through the *Automotive News* classifieds thinking about giving up and getting a job. I happened to look out in the backyard and there was a squirrel going out on a bare limb to reach a nut on the very end of the tiniest twig of a limb. This squirrel was determined on that winter day that he was going to reach that nut. He stretched himself out there, putting himself in danger of falling, just to reach that nut. I thought, that's me! I am convinced that God sent that squirrel to tell me, as Winston Churchill so famously said, "Never, never, never give up."

So with a renewed spirit and my trust in God, I finally convinced dealer after dealer to put their trust in me, and Tim Byrd & Associates became a successful F&I development company. Developing very profitable F&I departments was my specialty, and I became a trusted advisor to many car dealers. The world's greatest motivator and a fine Christian man, Zig Ziglar taught me that "you can have everything in life you want, if you will just help other people get what they want." With that in mind, finding ways to help my dealers be more profitable helped me become more valuable to my dealers.

As you can imagine, being a successful consultant and always looking for the best products available for my dealers has lead me to learn about many different warranty companies. The term "warranty company" in our business is a universal term to describe any company that provides vehicle service contracts, vehicle warranties, tire and wheel products, dent and ding products, theft products, environmental products, etc. I have always tried to represent the best and have knowledge of the rest. There are some very good third-party warranty companies out there. Companies that work very hard to provide the best service possible to dealerships and their customers. Others make big promises and underdeliver and are not adequately reserved. If you are serious about being a great dealer, and you probably wouldn't be reading this book if you were not, don't tarnish your reputation by selling something that is unrealistic just because it has a cheap price. Remember, the performance of the service contract you sell is a direct reflection on you and your dealership! With that being, said I am not writing this to sell you a warranty but to reveal to you a huge profit center that you are quite possibly, completely overlooking.

First, it is important you know the basics. All warranty companies are basically the same. What is covered is disclosed and priced, based on actuarial figures. That price dissected includes what we refer to as an "admin fee." The admin fee consists of fees to the administrator who administer the warranties and adjudicate claims, a fee to an insurance company to insure it, a fee to the agent, and a fee to the roadside assistance company. The total of the admin fee is usually 20 percent or less of the cost of the product. The balance of the cost of the warranty is the reserve, which is set aside to pay claims. What happens to that reserve is the major difference between warranty companies. Most warranty companies absorb any earned reserve (not used to pay claims) as profit. A warranty contract is earned based on the term. For example, a 12-month contract earns one-twelfth per month. Some warranty companies have what they call a retro or profit participation program. They will return a portion of the earned reserve to the dealer if the dealership produces X number of warranties and continues to do business with them. (So if the dealer sells the store, retires or falls below a volume requirement, the warranty company is not obligated to continue including the dealer in its profit share.) If the dealer does receive a profit share, they will also receive a 1099 from the warranty company on what is considered commission, normally having the highest tax consequences.

Every day in buy here, pay here, new and pre-owned operations, there are universal problems that all dealer's face. Mainly vehicles break down, and customers don't have the money for repairs, which equals upset customers and repossessed vehicles. The options I see most dealers choose include:

- *Buying a third-party warranty or service contract to sell to the customer.* This has its own problems. Laying out that upfront cash for a BHPH dealer can put a big dent in your lending pool and is expensive for all dealers. Dealers using a third-party warranty are faced with the fact that someone other than yourself is making the business decision of whether or not the repair for your customer is covered. If the claim is denied, you can beg, endure the frustration, put them on a side note or end up paying for it as good will if you want to keep the customer and not tarnish your reputation .

- *Setting money aside (reserve) and paying for repairs as they come up.* Sounds like a good idea—doing it yourself—but this reserve money must be counted as gross profit. Any money you set aside in an account or put in a drawer you will have to pay taxes on. You can reduce your expenses with your claims, but paying 35 percent or so on what's left of your reserve seems like an expensive way to go. So unless you are going to fly by the seat of your pants and just take 'em as they come, you need structure as well as reserve. What's covered, what's not, because if everything is covered with no parameters, you are by law implying a lifetime bumper-to-bumper warranty. In addition, keeping up with claims and accounting internally can be very difficult and labor intensive and only gets worse if your customer breaks down out of town.

- *Using the 50/50 method where you and the customer split the repair bill.* This might work for inexpensive claims, but again the customer is going to be required to come up with money, and we know how effective that plan is. That leaves you paying all or most of the bill (once again dipping into gross profit) or enduring a tarnished reputation or increased repossessions. This again raises the question, What happens if your customer breaks down out of town and out of your control?

Your best option is setting up a "dealer-owned reinsurance company." Turnkey, dealer-owned reinsurance companies are also known as producer-owned reinsurance companies, or 831(b) corporations, based on the Internal Revenue Code 831 (b). Reinsurance has been around for 30-plus years and was first used by larger dealers to reinsure credit life, accident and health insurance, and warranty/service contract products. Reinsurance companies are formed with minimal capitalization requirements.

By setting up a dealer-owned warranty company, you get all the benefits of a third-party warranty company via claims management and accounting: administrator obligor, structured coverage with roadside assistance including towing, and an 800 number for customers to call for nationwide coverage, with a professional claims team to look out for your best interest. When a claim occurs, the professional claims team will decide if the claim is covered, based on the warranty language initially agreed upon. You can custom design the coverage that is best for you and your customers. Another important difference from the third-party warranty for the BHPH dealer is that customers can finance the cost of the warranty with your warranty company. A prorated portion of the cost of the warranty is collected and forwarded to the dealer's reinsurance company trust account.

Reinsurance trust accounts, which are located in the United States, are just as indicated, a trust. Trusts are recognized as the safest place to keep money, and the dealer reinsurance trust account is not comingled but stands on its own. Trusts do not have checking accounts nor do they make loans to others, like a bank, with your money. The unearned premiums in a trust account can only be used as outlined in the trust agreement. In this case, to pay your customers claims.

The monies paid by the customer for their vehicle service contract (VSC) is set aside in reserve in your trust account, as I indicated above. Any reserve not used to pay claims becomes profit. As an example, if you sell an average of 20 vehicle service contracts per month, and $800 goes into reserve from each customer's VSC, loss ratios vary, but for this example let's say, $400 or 50 percent of every contract on average is used to pay claims. This leaves a $400 profit, which is $96,000 in additional dealer net profit per year and $480,000 additional dealer net profit at the end of five years. This does not include the retail profit made from the sale of the VSC. If you sell third-party vehicle service contracts now, the earned reserve is retained by the third-party warranty company as their profit, in this case, $96,000 per year.

Another very important benefit to owning your warranty company is tax benefits. I am not a CPA, but I know some good ones. They tell me in layman terms that these reinsurance companies are small property and causality companies. Small property and casualty insurance companies with less than $1.2 million in annual net premiums may elect to be taxed *only* on investment income under Internal Revenue Code 831 (b). Distributions are taxed at the dividend rate, currently 15 percent. These corporations, unlike S corporations or limited liability corporations (LLC) where income flows through to the shareholders annually, are C corporations. 831(b) C corporations allow the shareholder a more long-term approach. If a distribution is not desirable, you can retain the money in your reinsurance company, or you or your other business entities, may borrow money from your reinsurance company. 831(b) corporations make great retirement programs. Earned reserve can be invested in stocks, bonds or other securities within the trust account. 831(b) corporations make a great estate planning tool.

So, with a dealer-owned reinsurance company, you have nationwide warranty coverage, which is paid for by your customer, accounted as a dealership expense, saving you tax dollars on the dealership side and control over policy design, with a new profit center that is income-tax friendly, to say the least.

Warranties and VSC's are not the only products that can be reinsured. One which buy here pay here dealers may not be familiar with is voluntary debt cancellation coverage (DCC).

As used car values increase, I don't know of a BHPH dealer or finance company that does not want their customers to carry full coverage insurance. The problem arises when the customer allows that coverage to lapse, therefore putting into jeopardy the dealer or finance company's collateral. Industry research indicates that 50 percent of most BHPH books of business are uninsured. Customers put an average of $300 into insurance policies that they let lapse within 90 days, essentially throwing away that money. Many dealers have personnel assigned strictly for the purpose of making collection calls for the insurance companies who are reaping the financial gains off the dealer's man hours. Debt cancellation coverage is a product designed to relieve those problems and turn them into a profit center. By capturing the money the customer would be spending with the insurance company and ceding to your dealer-owned reinsurance company, DCC alleviates the need for you to require full coverage insurance. DCC puts you in control when there are claims. Instead of dealing with the insurance company, you have a professional claims team looking out for your best interest. DCC dealers have no unprotected collateral on the road and are not having to absorb uninsured losses. Buy here pay here dealers can usually provide a warranty on the car and DCC on the loan cheaper than the customer can buy insurance from their agent. So you profit from money that you had required the customer spend with someone else. This is not liability insurance required by state law. Since you make the collection calls on lapsed collateral coverage, doesn't it make sense to profit from it?

Not all dealers will see or hear of the benefits in unlocking the hidden profits of reinsurance, thus giving you an "Unfair Advantage." May God bless you in your business.

About Tim

Tim Byrd is founder and president of Tim Byrd & Associates Inc. located in Gloucester, Virginia. An auto industry expert on dealer-owned reinsurance companies and F&I development and a 25-plus-year veteran of the car business, Tim is a trusted advisor to many car dealers. Tim is married and has five beautiful children. Tim has been featured in *Virginia Independent News, Special Finance Insider, Around the Commonwealth* and *Dealer Business Journal.*

Website: www.timbyrd.net
Blog: www.timbyrd.net/blog
Facebook: www.facebook.com/reinsurance101
Twitter: www.twitter.com/TimByrdRE1
LinkedIn: www.linkedin.com/pub/tim-byrd/34/3b9/56a
Email: timbyrd@timbyrd.net
7488 Compromise Hill Rd.
Gloucester, VA 23061
Phone: (757) 532-3938 (main contact number)
Fax: (804) 693-6707

CHAPTER 12

What Car Dealerships Can Learn About Business and Branding from the Kardashians and Lady Gaga

By Tracy E. Myers, CMD

In today's celebrity-obsessed world, your chances of becoming rich and famous—or building a successful business are likely to depend more on your ability to build and promote a great brand than your talent or the service you offer.

We may not think this is the ideal state of affairs, but it's a harsh reality. It's equally true in business that the most successful companies in any market are often not those that have the best products and services but are those which are best at creating and managing brands.

Now I'm not saying that you should do anything other than offer the best products and services in your car dealership. But the truth is we can learn a lot from the celebrity world about how to become well-known and make money.

Take the Kardashian family, for example. Love them or hate them, the fact is they have become a multi-million-dollar moneymaking machine. Just in case you've managed to escape knowing who the Kardashians are, they're a family of socialites who have become reality TV stars. Their show "Keeping Up With the Kardashians" has aired over the past five years on the E! Network and is enormously popular. This has led to several spin-off shows featuring various members of the family. However their influence and income generation extends far beyond the TV shows. They have managed to monetize everything from a famous "leaked" sex tape to diet pills, fragrances and clothing lines.

The family may be simply "famous for being famous," but they have worked out how to make that highly profitable. Their licensing partnerships alone were said to have netted them more than $65 million in 2010. That's way beyond what many household-name stars, who are actually famous for their acting, music or sports skills, can achieve.

Let's face it, you and I probably won't get paid $100,000 to attend a store opening or get paid a huge sum just for sending out a short message to our Twitter followers, but there are several things we can learn from the way they work. So here are my Top 7 Kardashian Business Building Lessons for car dealers.

7 BUSINESS BUILDING LESSONS FROM THE KARDASHIANS

1. Give Your Market What They Want

The Kardashians understand what their target market is looking for. They know that it's partly about people aspiring to be rich and famous like them and getting a peak into their lifestyle. But they also know that people can identify with their everyday concerns and problems. So they make sure to share a picture of their luxury lifestyle as well as being open about their personal lives.

They don't care that lots of people don't like them or are bored by their constant appearance in the media. They cater only for their target market and ignore the rest.

One of the lessons we can learn from them is that trying to please everyone means we please no one. So think about what you can do to focus more on your ideal customer rather than trying to make everyone happy.

2. Tailor Your Brand to Different Needs

One of the factors that boost the Kardashians' moneymaking power is that there are several members of the family and each appeals to different people. This extends their reach beyond what one could achieve alone.

Along with branding the entire family, they make use of each as individual as a brand and profit center. In this way, they cover a wide demographic.

To learn from this, consider how you can present a slightly different face to different markets in your dealership, such as young singles, families or seniors within a consistent overall brand.

3. Make Your Brand Reach As Far As It Can

The Kardashians may have begun with a foray into retail as owners of the DASH clothing chain, but their brand has now extended into a wide range of areas such as lifestyle clothing, fragrances, diet supplements, and even a "celebrity destination" store in Las Vegas.

Knowing their core market demographic, they have been able to find many different ways of reaching the same market. Of course, this can be pushed too far, and the Kardashians have made mistakes such as a deal with a pre-paid credit card that was viewed as offering a poor deal for customers. Nevertheless, the idea of stretching your brand into new areas where you can serve your customers is worth careful thought.

4. Harness the Power of Social Media

The success of the Kardashians is proof of the power of social media, such as Facebook and Twitter, in growing a fan base of people ready to buy. For example, they have millions of Twitter followers, which provide a strong market for their own products and for promoting others.

They go for it 100 percent and share a lot of themselves in social media. You probably won't want to open up your private life in the way the Kardashians do, but sharing a bit of yourself in social media can help build a better relationship with your customers. You can also use social media to enhance your position as an informed industry expert, sharing your expertise and giving valuable information.

5. Build Success Through Partnerships

The Kardashian success is built on partnerships with other successful brands, whether those are businesses or individuals. They can enhance their own celebrity through connections with other celebrities. They can also buy themselves credibility through association with established respected businesses. And, of course, partnership offers the opportunity for them to move quickly into markets where they have no expertise.

So think about how you can use partnership with others—either through endorsement or working together—to expand what you offer to your customers or to reach new markets.

6. Learn and Profit From Your Mistakes

The Kardashians have been successful at taking advantage when things go wrong. They managed to earn millions when someone else released Kim's famous sex tape. When one of them puts on weight, they make a fortune by losing it and sharing their secrets of how they did it.

We all get things wrong in business sometimes, and we should aim to learn from those mistakes to improve what we do. It can even be an opportunity to build better relationships.

7. Know Your Strengths

The big advantage the Kardashians have is that they are attractive and have charisma, so they make the most of these attributes. When they promote clothes, jewelry, makeup and shoes, they look good and make the products look good. That makes potential buyers believe they would look good in them too , so they go out and buy them.

They are smart enough to steer clear of activities that don't make the best of their strengths, though they also know how to partner with people who can make up for their weaknesses. It's a good idea to take time to work out your own strengths or those of your dealership and then focus on them. There is likely to be something that you do better than others, and that can be a key part of your brand. When you share this with others, you want them to see you as the "go to" dealership in your area.

Those are some of the lessons we can learn about business from the Kardashian family. However, the best-known member of the family is Kim, and there are separate lessons she can teach us about how to build a strong personal brand that stands out from the rest.

7 PERSONAL BRANDING LESSONS FROM KIM KARDASHIAN

1. Take Time to Build Relationships

One of the highest profile events for Kim was the build-up to her wedding with basketball player Kris Humphries and the subsequent problems arising from the marriage that lasted only 72 days till she filed for divorce. They got engaged after just six months and went in to a very high-profile wedding, which some saw as a fairly cynical business move. But whatever the truth behind the marriage, she quickly discovered there was no basis for a lasting relationship.

The same is true in business. Good customer relationships are not based on a single meeting or the first sale but are built over many years. A good customer relationship is worth a lot over a lifetime, so it's worth investing time to make sure your customers keep coming back.

2. Act Fast When Necessary

One positive lesson coming out of the short-lived marriage was the importance of acting quickly when you see things aren't working out. At least Kim acted quickly when it was clear the marriage was not going to last.

We can often benefit from that lesson in business and follow the maxim of "hire slow, fire fast." Too many businesses carry employees that are not effective, but we often delay firing them because we don't want to admit we made a mistake or we don't want to take away someone's livelihood.

But how much is this ineffective employee costing you and what problems are they causing for the rest of your staff? Never let one person get in the way of the performance of the whole team or stop you delivering the right service to your customers.

3. Communicate When Things Go Wrong

As soon as the divorce was announced, many claimed she had only gone through with the wedding for money. So her mother, Kris Jenner, gave lots of interviews claiming that Kim had married out of love and did not make millions from the wedding.

Not everyone was convinced and managing these risks is much easier if you behave with integrity all the way through. However, in a world of

24/7 news with instant social media reaction, there are no secrets. You have to be willing to explain yourself and answer questions.

Kim went on "The Tonight Show" with Jay Leno and said, "I learned so many lessons, and it's changed who I am as a person—I think for the better." She claimed to have been shocked about the media reaction to the breakup, so perhaps she believed too much of her own publicity.

When things go wrong in your business, be honest about the situation and take responsibility for putting it right as fast as possible. This can go a long way to getting people back on your side and even strengthening the relationship.

4. Perception Is Everything

Good brands that take a long time to build can be ruined overnight based on what people believe about you, whether their belief is true or not. No matter the arguments Kim and her mother made, many people felt the wedding was some kind of peep-show where everyone was duped into believing the story and then felt ripped off when it all fell apart so quickly.

You can avoid this sort of action if you are always seen to act with your customers' best interests at heart.

Bear in mind that a cheap publicity stunt or cutting corners on service may get you a short-term outcome but is unlikely to pay off in the long run.

To keep on top of people's perceptions, you need to track what people think about you and your business. This allows you to take action to correct any misleading impressions out there. You can track perception by doing surveys and also by tracking online comments through resources such as Google Alerts.

If you find online reviews about your business that you don't agree with, make sure you react appropriately. First, you need to address whatever issue is being raised. You also need to work hard to make sure that people who are satisfied with your service write positive reviews.

Always remember your brand is driven by what other people are saying about you and not what you say about yourself.

5. Be Passionate About What You Do

Kim may be lucky that she is able to make money from promoting clothes, shoes, jewelry and perfumes. It's easy to feel good about that when you look great.

But there's no reason why we can't all bring that kind of passion to our businesses. We should be proud of what we offer, and be ready to talk about it positively all the time.

We need to be our own best cheerleaders with a genuine pride in what we offer our customers. Letting your enthusiasm speak for itself will keep your brand strong and help your business prosper long term.

6. Be Seen in the Right Places

Whether it's going to the right nightclubs or building a big following on Facebook and Twitter, Kim wants to be seen with the right people and be talked about. You should be the same in your business, but instead of the nightclubs maybe you need to be seen in the local mall or at charity events.

At the same time, you should put some effort into building a presence on top social networking sites like Facebook, Twitter, Google+ and LinkedIn. But don't just make it a presence; participate so that you are seen as a valued member of these communities.

7. Don't Be Afraid to Build Hype

A lot of successful marketing is about building interest in things in advance. When you build anticipation before you launch something, people become excited about it. Learn from the way trailers for movies appear many months in advance to build up anticipation.

Of course the last thing you want is to create hype and then fail to deliver on the "promise," as Kim did with her wedding. However, most people go to the opposite extreme and hide their light under a bushel.

If you have a major event coming up in your dealership, such as a new launch or a special sale, get people interested and excited in advance.

These are a few personal branding secrets we can learn from Kim, but the Kardashian family are not the only celebrities we can learn from. Many of today's celebrities demonstrate attributes you can apply in your business. Another great role model is New York singer Lady Gaga.

LADY GAGA'S MARKETING SECRETS

Although she is a very talented performer, what makes Lady Gaga stand out is her outrageous costumes and elaborate staging. Her shows are not simply performances; they are striking events that are truly memorable. This has made her into a personality that stretches way beyond her music and means she is featured in the media regularly. What can we learn from Lady Gaga when it comes to the marketing and branding of your dealership?

1. Dare to Be Different
Although she's a very talented singer, Lady Gaga realized right from the early days of her career that she needed to find a way to stand out. She figured that meant being a performer, not just a singer. This led her to craft an outrageous persona. If you want to stand out from your competition, you need to figure out what you can add to your offer or to the way you work to make you memorable and attract more customers.

2. Engage Your Fans and Customers
Lady Gaga realizes that being different isn't enough to sustain a relationship with her fans (her ultimate customers). One of the ways she keeps them engaged is through social networking platforms such as Facebook, where she is one of the top personalities with more than 50 million likes. She uses this as part of the way of building a brand through genuine communication. She affectionately refers to her 10 million-plus Twitter followers as "little monsters."

How can you use social media to engage your customers and expand your target market? Are you posting regularly to build relationships and create new ones?

3. Keep Moving Forward
With Lady Gaga, it was not simply a matter of coming up with an identity and dressing up that way.

She knows her fans expect her to keep on developing, so she continues to improve her offer. She is always looking for new ways to express her talents and to make her shows and her music more outrageous and appealing.

In your business, you have to be careful not to get complacent. The pace of change now means that if you are not moving forward, you are moving backward. There is no standing still.

4. Build On Core Beliefs and Values

Part of the Lady Gaga appeal is that she has not been created by someone else. She is not some manufactured personality. She had a concept of what she wanted to do through her music, and she lives that constantly. Her fans have come to expect something special of her, and she does not disappoint them.

In the same way, you build the success of your business on strong foundations when you have genuine concern about the way you serve your customers. When you stray from these values, you make bad decisions and customers have fewer reasons to stay with you.

5. Keep Your Customers Satisfied

Lady Gaga makes a promise to deliver a memorable performance, and she delivers on that promise consistently every time, whether on stage, in video, in audio or in person. She also stays focused on her music and rarely tarnishes her brand by appearing in the news for the wrong reasons. She knows what her customers want, and she keeps giving them more.

Remember that your brand is your promise to your customers, so make sure you always deliver on it.

6. Build Partnerships and Leverage Your Brand

While Lady Gaga has a highly distinctive product, she knows she can reach new audiences by collaborating with other performers. Her own strong brand attracts others to work with her, and this can take her beyond music into involvement in other products and services. Think about who you can work with to add new services or reach new markets.

7. Find New Ways to Reach Your Target Market

Lady Gaga has led the way in using new media, such as YouTube, to reach her audience. She was the first performer to reach 1 billion hits on her YouTube videos. Her striking performances made her a natural for this media.

So think about what different ways you can use to reach your target market. It doesn't have to be high-tech options such as YouTube; it could be a free white paper that you offer on your website. It's just finding places your competitors won't be so you can get your message across to the right people.

Between the Kardashians and Lady Gaga, we can learn a great deal from celebrities about growing a successful business. It may be tempting to see these celebrities as living in a world detached from everyday life and having no relevance to the challenges of running a business. However, when you realize that many of these people are really successful businesses in their own right, you can spot many lessons that you can apply to your dealership.

Applying these techniques can give you an Unfair Advantage over your competition by helping you become a celebrity in your market and by building a large group of fans who will happily follow you as customers for a very long time.

About Tracy

Tracy Myers is commonly referred to as The Nation's Premier Automotive Solutions Provider. Best-selling author and legendary speaker Brian Tracy called him "a visionary to be compared to a Walt Disney for a new generation."

He is also a Certified Master Dealer and was the youngest ever recipient of the National Quality Dealer of the Year award by the NIADA, which is the highest obtainable honor in the used car industry. His car dealership, Frank Myers Auto Maxx, was recently recognized as the No. 1 Small Business in North Carolina by *Business Leader Magazine,* one of the Top 3 dealerships to work for in the country by *The Dealer Business Journal*, and one of the Top 22 Independent Automotive Retailers in the United States by *Auto Dealer Monthly Magazine*.

Myers has been a guest business correspondent on FOX News, appeared on NBC, ABC and CBS affiliates across the country, featured in *USA Today*, and written for *Fast Company*. His inspirational stories and strategies for success are in demand across the country, which has given him the opportunity to share the stage with the likes of with Zig Ziglar, James Malinchak, Brian Tracy, Mike Koenig, Bob Burg and Tom Hopkins, just to name a few. His best-selling books help people become better consumers as well as inspire industry leaders to become "game changers." He was also featured in the five-time Telly Award-Winning film "Car Men."

As the founder of his own marketing and branding academy, Tracy teaches ambitious business owners, professionals and entrepreneurs how to get noticed, gain instant credibility, make millions and dominate their competition.

For more information about Tracy Myers, please visit www.TracyMyers.com.

CHAPTER 13

Technology Is Here to Stay— Jump on the Bandwagon or Fall Behind

By Glen Garvin, Group General Manager, Dominion Dealer Solutions

When I look back on all the pieces of technology I have owned or used, I can remember them all pretty well. I remember the Apple IIe in my parents' house, my first Compaq Contura 4/25 laptop, my first enormous digital camera, my first TiVo. But strangely, I have a hard time remembering the phone I carried before my first iPhone; I am pretty sure it was a flip phone. The lack of recollection is particularly impactful because I made the purchase just four years ago. Such is the shelf life of life-changing technology.

Like much technology, smartphones were initially just a luxury item, something to show off to your friends. But quickly they have become necessities. In fact, a January 2012 Nielsen study shows us that smartphone adoption rates among the younger generation are growing rapidly, even among those just above the poverty line. Within the past three months, new subscribers, aged 18 to 34, are ordering smartphones eight out of 10 times.

There is no question that mobile devices will continue to grow market share and continue to evolve until the next piece of revolutionary

133

technology replaces them. The imperative is how to harness this technology to embrace those customers who use it as their primary means of communication and consumption.

In this chapter, you will learn about:

- the importance of smartphone technology in the United States today

- the value of mobile phone "apps"

- recent emergence of QR codes

- ways to leverage these tools for your dealership

HOW DID WE GET MOBILE?

One of the most important things to remember is that consumers will always adopt technology faster than most businesses, including automobile dealers. The earliest consumer adopters and innovators already expect and use social information, apps and QR codes. They are using their social sphere and reviews as part of their everyday decision-making process. They are already seeking out new technologies, such as augmented reality, as the next wave to use their smartphones.

I am predicting that augmented reality, while still probably a year away, is going to be the newest rendition of QR codes that will change the landscape of on-site marketing. Think of it this way: QR codes most commonly provide information through a pre-programmed URL destination, while augmented reality allows a true interaction where the environment is combined with advertising in an interactive way. Want an example? The first real-life example is the "first-down" line in a football game, where the line enhances the game for the viewer but is an "overlay" on top of the reality. Remember how amazed you were when you first saw the first down marker? Prepare yourself for the immense marketing opportunities that will come. Imagine a wristwatch that you can hold over your wrist to check to see how it would look and flip through colors, faces and bands…the possibilities are endless.

If you remember that the auto dealer is human and that his expertise is marketing automobiles, then you have to wonder how he is going to keep up with the rapid rate of technological advancement, let alone use it to his advantage? It seems almost unfair for salespeople, dealership management or owners to be expected to do so. Whoever thought the car business would become so technical? Try this experiment: Think about the first dealership you remember with a website? How is their business today? I will be willing to bet that the earliest adopters in websites have continued to be the early adopters of technology at all levels and are probably leading the way with mobile solutions as well.

To understand how innovation impacts the product life cycle, let's take a closer look at "Roger's Diffusion of Innovation" graph shown below. A typical product life cycle spans four distinct areas: introduction, growth, maturity and decline. As a product is launched into the market, consumers adopt the technology at the pace that best suits their needs and desires. Most new products will attract a small percentage of the population as innovators and adopters. The majority of consumers will fall in the large part of the bell curve as early to late majority. These consumers are constantly landscaping new technology and waiting for others to recommend the best solutions. The last type of consumer is the laggards. Once a technology has hit its maturity level in the market, businesses will see laggards finally jump on board.

The good news is that just by virtue of reading this, you are already exposing yourself to innovation and exploring ideas on how you can beat your competitors to the punch with these mobile marketing strategies.

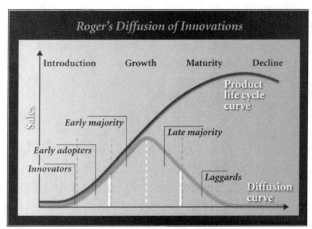

Courtesy: 2008, AEGIS Publication LLC

However, the reality remains. The majority of dealerships fall into late majority in adoption and will struggle with the inherent process changes at their dealership. If you can be at the forefront of the innovation cycle by introducing new technological strategies, including process implementation changes, you can meet the expectations and ride the wave of the product life cycle with your customers. Small changes with the latest technology will lead auto dealers to higher profits through both front-end and back-end revenue growth.

We have established that a majority of your customers will leverage a mobile device in their decision-making process and that it is beneficial for your dealership to be part of the early adoption cycle to beat your competitors and fulfill needs of consumers ready to harness mobile technology. Next, we will look at some ways that you can create a tangible mobile strategy.

CREATE A DEALERSHIP APP

Mobile web is important. It is critical for your dealership's website to render and function appropriately on mobile devices. Dealerships that leverage adaptive website design, which renders pages based on the type of device being used by the consumer, will improve the customer's web experience. Adaptive websites not only thoughtfully display a website to a consumer based on the type of device but also serve up a customized experience based on a consumer's surfing history. However, you need to think beyond a mobile website. You need to strategically plan how to capture a piece of real estate on the consumer's phone. You need an app on the smartphone.

Your branded app must provide the customer with tangible benefits in order for them to want it. The app must help make their life easier and show real value to maintain valuable space on their smartphone. Think about your life as a consumer. What functions on your phone would make the most sense for you to leverage on a regular basis? Would you download an app if you could confidently schedule a service appointment without any phone calls, emails or correspondence with the dealership? What if you could access your own vehicles' service history and practical vehicle information or receive service recall alerts automatically? From your own business perspective, could you improve your "show rate" if your dealership's app delivered service appointment reminders the day before an appointment on their phone?

The utilization impact of these tools is vital in retention of your customer base. Relationships formerly were the key driver for return purchases and service adoption, but the consumer does not have to rely on the salesperson or service advisor any longer. Sophisticated tools, like a dealer app, are expected. These tools can keep your customer engaged with open lines of communication. Don't confine your app to tools that only benefit you. In order to survive tomorrow, you need to think like a consumer and meet their needs in ways that do not traditionally seem like natural moneymakers. For instance, you may think that a mobile phone app with a button for a flashlight or a parking spot reminder is foolish. However, it is just like that branded pen you hand out at your cashier desk. Every time the consumer uses that flashlight or parking spot reminder, he/she will be reminded of your dealership and brand. It is another way of strategically using technology to promote your brand and dealership.

These tools are available today but are only being used by the bleeding-edge car dealers. Be careful to understand this point: *Apps have been available for years, but they have not served consumers' needs.* The newer generation of apps serve the consumer with useful and practical applications.

As with any new process or tool, train your customer-facing employees about your website, mobile technology tools and advertising. This is true for all forms of technology but vitally important for mobile technology. If you are not a user of mobile technology, you will have difficulty relating to those who do. Have you ever seen an uninformed salesperson demonstrate a piece of technology in the car when they have never used it?

Some of the most popular forms of apps today are location-based apps. You may be familiar with tools such as Foursquare, which allows users to "check-in" at locations and qualify for points and even special services. It is critical that you educate your staff about any special services offered through these portals. Users of location-based check-in apps can undoubtedly tell stories of trying to redeem a coupon or special only to meet the gaze of a clerk, hostess or receptionist who is unaware of the special, or worse, the mobile technology that features it. If dealers can get this right, they can create immense customer loyalty with incredibly low effort. Each location-based service (LBS) is different, but let's take Foursquare as an example. A dealer needs to simply claim their location, then offer simple specials. Make sure to set up notifications of people checking in. When dealers see those check-ins and take action (as simple as just greeting them to say hi), you will be amazed at the loyalty that develops.

Let me give you an example I faced a couple of years ago. After purchasing a vehicle with a mobile technology package that included an integrated Bluetooth mic and sound, I was initially told it wouldn't pair with the iPhone. However, prior to leaving the dealership, the salesperson took my phone and tried to fumble through screens for several minutes before I told him to forget it. Would I download that dealers' app based on the recommendation of that salesperson? No way! The salesperson has to be credible in related technology. They must understand consumer behavior, and they must be competent with the technology.

QR CODES AND THE SHOPPING EXPERIENCE

New cars are rolling off the assembly line with QR codes on their OEM window sticker, but less than 20 percent of dealerships are using QR codes on their used vehicle window stickers. The average dealer leveraging QR codes is getting utilization of 40 scans per month. This example again demonstrates how consumers outpace dealerships in technology adoption. Consumers are looking for these 3-D digital boxes on advertising materials, like used car window stickers, to get more information and help them with their decision-making process. They will turn away from dealers that do not offer the information and transparency they expect.

When consumers are close to a decision on a vehicle but choose not to purchase, there are likely several reasons behind that behavior. Aside from financial reasons, a typical consumer pauses the buying process for fear of making a bad decision. That usually boils down to not having enough of the right information. Many tools exist online to facilitate the learning process, but not many are available on mobile devices.

Typically, the fear of a bad decision fits into one of these categories:

- ***Buying a bad car:*** What was the previous owner like? What has the car been put through? Will there be large future repairs? Has the vehicle been in any accidents or damaged in some way?

- ***Paying too much:*** Am I getting a good deal? How do I know? Will my neighbor pay less? Am I overspending?

- ***Buyer's remorse:*** What if I don't like it? What if I don't like the color? What if something goes wrong?

How can you use mobile technology to give your dealership an advantage to prevent these questions from haunting a consumer on your lot or on your web page? Here are a few ways you can use mobile technology and QR codes to your advantage:

- Link a QR code on your window sticker to the Carfax report.

- Link a QR code to the warranty description of the vehicle.

- Empower a salesperson to show comparative pricing instantly from their Apple iPad.

- Offer a dealership-branded mobile app that shows the complete service history of a vehicle.

- Link a QR code on your advertising and/or window stickers to your dealership's return policy or guaranteed trade-in offers video.

CUSTOMER REVIEWS

An entire chapter ("Online Reviews and Moldy Hotels") is already devoted to how today's consumer uses their social sphere to influence their buying decisions. Are you being specifically strategic in using mobile technology for collecting feedback and reviews? Are you making it easy for your customer to leave a review and to interact electronically within your dealership?

What else do progressive, cutting-edge dealerships offer? Simple stuff like offering Wi-Fi at your dealership is easy. Make that investment effective by promoting Wi-Fi availability with simple instructions, like username and password, and connecting instructions. Perhaps most important, empower your customer-facing employees with simple

FAQs about how to use these features. For example, I was recently at a dealership that had three wireless signals branded with their dealership. While waiting in the service department, I tried using it, and it was appropriately locked down with a password. I went to the receptionist to inquire about the password, but she did not even know they offered Wi-Fi. I then tried the service reception desk, but the clerk did not have the password either. Moral of this story? Train your staff about technology.

LESSONS LEARNED

This chapter is filled with information, and yet this is the tip of the iceberg. My goal was to educate you about the relevance and power of smartphone technology and give you some tips on how to leverage this technology for your business. A few tips worth remembering include:

- Become a smartphone owner and user.
- Require that your marketing plans include mobile-based websites and a dealership-branded app with user-friendly features.
- Begin using QR codes on your used vehicle window stickers and marketing literature.
- Train your customer-facing staff about your new tools.

Successful organizations watch their customers' behavior and adapt to meet their needs. Accessible technology has driven big changes to automotive operations and marketing. If you have ever followed the story of Suzuki of Wichita, you can see the power of an organization that is galvanized around technology. Everyone in that dealership embraces technology, uses it and explores it. In fact, it is so much a part of the dealership DNA and team dynamic that it is not an effort. This open-minded approach fosters new ideas and technology and allows the Wichita team to operate in the "blue ocean" where business is less competitive and more profitable.

You can be sure of one thing: As soon as you feel like you have caught up, the consumer will already be a couple steps ahead of you. Just keep at it, and ideas that seem foreign to you today, like "augmented reality," will be familiar and baked in to your operations and marketing plan.

About Glen

Glen has been with Dominion Enterprises since his business was acquired in 2000. Starting as an account representative, Glen eventually became a partner in the Rolling Maronie franchise prior to the acquisition by Dominion. He relocated to Jacksonville, Florida, and was instrumental in transitioning the companies' absorption into Dealer Specialties in 2002. In 2005, Dealer Specialties consolidated offices, and Glen played a key role in transitioning the company-owned operation from Florida to Monroe, Ohio, to put all of Dealer Specialties under one roof. Glen was the East Coast general manager before being promoted in 2006 to general manager of Dealer Specialties. Prior to working with Rolling Maronie, Glen worked for Aztec Systems, which did the data aggregation and compilation for the Zagat Restaurant Survey from 1985 until 1993.

Glen graduated from the Maxwell School of Management at Syracuse University with a degree in Business Administration. Glen and his family reside in Mason, Ohio.

CHAPTER 14

In the Driver's Seat: Be in Control of Your Own Website Managing Your Digital Assets

By Chuck Fisher

Recently, I was called into a franchise dealership to assist with a digital emergency. No, a hacker did not break into the dealer's DMS and rob the dealership data. The matter was serious, and one that I see far too often.

The dealership had contracted with a full-service media group, which had handled their website, mailers, and TV spots. After months of poor performance, the dealer decided to terminate their agreement.

Not understanding the full impact of this decision, the dealer created an emergency situation to which I was called in to help. Their website was immediately taken down by the terminated vendor. Existing digital advertising had phone numbers that were now directed back to the ad agency and not the dealership. Ouch!

Their internet presence was evaporated, and the dealership was officially an internet ghost. They no longer had a website, and no backup plan in place. I am not kidding when I stress that no one at the dealership even had a password to take control of the dealership domains.

To say it was a mess would be the understatement of the year. Regardless of a dealer's knowledge or comfort level with digital marketing, all dealers need a digital management plan in place.

In this case, it is obvious that there was no understanding about the repercussions of a cancelled digital contract that included web hosting. In this chapter, I will share my recommendations to prevent this story or a variation of it repeating at your dealership.

I will also challenge readers to take more responsibility for their digital assets, which includes an investment in inspecting and maintaining their websites, social media accounts, blogs and video marketing accounts.

KEEP YOUR DOMAINS UNDER YOUR CONTROL

Own and control all your domain names. That is my first and foremost tip for any dealership. Know exactly where they are registered. Have all login information and passwords in a central file. Create an email account that is connected to the domain ownership account so you can get notices when domains are expiring.

How can you own an office building and not have a key to get in? Would you allow someone to change the locks on all the doors and not give you a key?

This is not a Chuck Norris movie, and we don't need any hostage situations. Hostile business relationships only cause delays, which cost dealers time and money. Even if a best friend of the dealership is the vendor hired to build or manage the dealership's website, the business needs to have primary control and access.

Despite the demands of the website vendor, dealers can control their domains in their own account and just point them to their web and email servers. Companies have been known to play games when it comes to money or losing a client. Don't put the dealership in that situation!

After I took control of the domain for the aforementioned dealer, I created a new domain account for the dealer principal, someone who was going to be there all the time.

DESIGNATE THE RESPONSIBILITY

What I discovered was there was not one single person properly trained to handle the digital assets for the dealership. In fact, there are many cases where former employees who were trusted to manage digital accounts leave the dealership without passing on account information.

Does this sound familiar?

Dealer: Who has the login for Google+ Local? I just got back from a 20 Group, and want to change the settings on our listing.

Internet Manager: I don't have it. Joe created that account last year for us.

Dealer: Joe who?

Internet Manager: The college intern that helped us last year with SEO.

Dealer: Well do you know how to get in touch with him?

Internet Manager: No, I think he moved out of state.

Dealers spend thousands of dollars each month on advertising and rely heavily on their website and technology infrastructure. However, few take the time to assign responsibility to someone inside the dealership to document and manage their assets.

It's not uncommon for multiple employees and vendors to have a portion of the logins, passwords, and/or technical access to dealership systems. In most cases, whoever has the security access is not documented.

Dealers are pretty much handing the keys to their business to their vendors without any concerns. That's nuts! How can dealers let an outside party have total control of the company's digital assets and not have a spare key?

In this case, the dealer lost control because they had no process to manage their domains or control their email accounts. All their emails for service, parts and sales divisions were down when I arrived! Restoring email was crucial, since so much business today comes though email.

Dealers looking for an Unfair Advantage have to make sure their primary and secondary digital assessments are stable, managed and bullet proof. Have you checked when your domains are expiring?

DIGITAL MANAGERS NEED TRAINING

You have heard the saying "You only know, what you know!" That applies to dealership employees who are responsible for the company's digital assets, CRM processes and digital marketing investments. How can dealership employees inspect vendors and reports, and see if the dealership is potentially exposed without proper training?

Dealers need to invest in their staff by sending them to training. Dealers have to build a team that can take over and lend a hand if anything like this ever happens. Dealers need to develop a team that is knowledgeable in the key aspects of digital operations like website operations and maintenance, CRM configuration and workflows, and digital advertising. It should not be only one person in the store.

There are number of annual conferences and boot camps that can provide the training dealers need to insure their businesses against digital sabotage. Avoid the pitfall of sending one person, year after year. Don't put all your eggs in one basket.

Dealers need to have someone in the "family" who they can trust with a knowledge and passion for technical and digital operations. It is common sense, plain and simple. But since even family can disappoint, make sure you have backup!

DON'T BITE OFF MORE THAN YOU CAN CHEW

Have you considered how many products are in a dealer's digital library that are being invoiced month after month regardless if they are being used? If you work at a dealership, do you know when the last thorough audit was made in conjunction with the staff that actually uses the products under contract?

Assuming you control your emails, unlike the dealership story I opened with, how many products do you really use each day? I find more and more that dealers think they need multiple digital products, yet they are at a loss to share with me how these new investments will be measured for effectiveness.

At times dealership executives and managers let their eyes and imagination get the best of them. We all have experience with impulse buying. We may find ourselves salivating over a broad range of product offerings presented by a vendor. In an ideal world, it would be great to be able to implement everything the salesperson had to offer.

The reality is that most dealership employees never use the full set of tools that is purchased. Training or lack of training is a part of the problem. Accountability plays another part in failed utilization. Employees often stick with what is comfortable for them, or even in some cases they bail on the whole solution and go back to a pseudo manual process.

Dealers need to focus on the basics before they take on the technological world with everything that looks shiny and new. Be realistic on how fast your staff can assimilate change. Don't buy into the package deal if it will take a year to use all the features. You should be making the rules, not your vendor.

For example, don't buy your sales staff all new iPads if they won't access their email or use the CRM system regularly from their desktop devices. If your email and CRM system is not designed for the iPad, what efficiencies will you really get?

What about social media? Dealers want to jump in the pool, but once again, they need to have an account management in place and a strategy. You might hear a manager come back from a social media conference all excited and exclaim:

> "I am going to start a dealership Twitter account and update our Facebook account with a contest. I just signed us up for YouTube so I can post videos on our website. And by the way, we need to get on Foursquare, and we need a Pinterest account ASAP!"

Dealers need to funnel the passion and energy of their team in an orderly way. Digital assets will get totally messed up if there is no plan and process to manage them. Training and accountability must be part of the budget to ensure success.

Dealers who want an Unfair Advantage are aggressive but are also realistic on how much they can change, assimilate, and implement in any given month.

TECHNOLOGY IS MAKING ASSET MANAGEMENT EASIER

I hear over and over from dealer principals and their employees, "I'm tired of everyone trying to sell me something, I want them to show me how to do it!"

With the current website technology and widget-based solutions, dealers are becoming able to gain full control of their web pages and their URL structures. Website tools allow dealership staff to drag and drop pretty much anything they want on their website pages. This kind of technology makes a junior webmaster out of the most novice user.

In fact, at the 2012 NADA Convention, Cobalt announced their Flex

Website technology that allows dealers to drag and drop elements to their website pages and transform their websites in minutes. I personally have helped dealers create platforms that are easy to design, manage and update. I believe this trend will transform our industries' ability to design compelling websites.

As a result of better web publishing tools, progressive dealers may reduce their outsourcing of social media and content development. Dealers, when given the choice, may hire people with journalism backgrounds to create the unique content and imagery. If the search engines are leaning toward rewarding original content and frequent publishing activity, dealers may have to turn to internal staff to accomplish higher search authority.

Imagine the possibilities when you establish a staff position who can use this technology to be able to click on any page and make the changes you want. Those changes can include color palettes, banners, videos, or any customization that enhances your marketing strategy. The days of having an excuse for outdated specials pages are quickly coming to an end.

If you have a new sales campaign starting, widget-based website platforms will allow dealers to create landing pages quickly and effectively. The right combination of technology and staff training can make the potential of driving more to your dealership a reality.

For example, it is St. Patty's Day and a dealership is painting the town virtually green. The dealer may want to update banners, website colors and marketing messages. Having to wait on a vendor partner to schedule these updates will often result in being a day late and a dollar short.

Dealers that want an Unfair Advantage need agile website solutions and a properly trained staff. It all works very well together when a dealership has a complete plan to manage their digital assets.

MANAGING YOUR CONTRACTS

I have been in dealerships where you mention the word contracts and the executive team wants to run or hide. For the services I offer to dealers, I never ask them to sign a contract. If the dealership is not pleased with my work, why should I hold them captive?

I understand the nature of contracts and why they are used today. As part of a digital asset management plan, contract start and end dates should be clearly documented. Notes should be made if contract termination needs 30, 60, or 90-day advance notice. Read the fine print to see if contracts auto renew if cancellation notice is not given.

There are flexible and powerful technology solutions that do not require long-term contracts. How do you feel when a product you like demands a long-term contract before you have had any experience working with the company?

It's just like signing up to buy a cell phone. I ask myself, Why do I need a contract? Mr. Cell Phone Company, why do you need to lock me in for two years? Are you just going to forget me once you have my money?

Dealers who want an Unfair Advantage carefully read and negotiate their contracts so that they can be nimble to change as the market changes. Vendor partners that fail to deliver on their promises do not hold these dealers back.

If a dealer can walk away from a contract by giving 30 days notice, will that keep a vendor on their toes? If a dealer can't walk away easily, then what motivates a vendor to deliver high customer service? Dealers must address these questions.

Minimal contracts, such as ones with three- to six-months terms are reasonable, but today, one-year contracts just seem excessive. I work with many dealerships that don't like the performance they are getting from their online vendors.

They lament, "There is nothing I can do, I am in a contract." What they don't realize is a website or product that is hindering performance and sales, most likely is costing the dealership more in lost opportunity than what they are paying each month.

PERSONAL NOTE

There is the old saying, "If you want something done right, you have to do it yourself." This is true to a point, but dealers need the right resources to train their staff and the guidance to select products that will serve their dealership well.

Don't hand over the keys to the castle! Learn how to manage your digital assets and partner with quality vendors when your internal skill sets are not sufficient. Allowing a dealership to be shut down through lack of understanding and/or execution is not an acceptable outcome for entrepreneurial dealer principals.

About Chuck

Chuck Fisher is the CEO of Rank My Media LLC, a multichannel marketing firm based in Outer Banks, North Carolina. Chuck's internet background includes more than 30 years in the industry. His career has almost spanned the life of the world wide web.

With his knowledge in lead generation—from business development on the manufacturing side to distribution and setting up call center environments—he understands all dynamics of the modern marketing world.

Leaving his innovative imprint on the current market, Chuck has worked with America's top franchises and still remains entrenched in many industries today. He has watched and projected many of the changes that are currently being implemented in today's dealer solutions.

Chuck has collaborated and developed a progressive widget-based dealer website solution allowing the user full control of the design, URL, link structure and all other parameters. This allows the dealership to modify their online presence using agile deployment from their own staff. The program encourages car dealers to use multiplatform deployment with social networking and consistency of online branding to leverage a website to enhance sales.

Rank My Media provides online venues and processes, and allows dealers the opportunity to create webmasters in-house for swift changes—no more relying on outside vendors that require contracts and take your money for little or no results.

Chuck is a member of the CIADA Association to promote and resource Independent Automobile Dealers in North Carolina and South Carolina.

For more information about Chuck Fisher or Rank My Media,
visit www.rankmymedia.com.

CHAPTER 15

Creating an Executive Dashboard

By Brian Pasch

Dealers are inundated with reports from their vendors. A recent survey I conducted on the Automotive Digital Marketing (ADM) community revealed that dealers are reviewing at least 20 different reports each month for marketing and operational partners.

If you're currently working at a dealership, do you feel overwhelmed with the number of reports you receive each month? Since there are no standards for data reporting, automotive professionals must attempt to organize, compare and chart progress showing an expected return on investment (ROI) from their ventures. For many dealers, the task is just too time consuming, so reports are only intensely reviewed during a fire drill.

You may have experienced the fire drill in your line of work. It normally starts with a phone call from an excited executive who thinks that a particular vendor's product or service isn't delivering the expected ROI. Reports are requested and an urgent meeting called. In most cases, the reports don't have enough data or data that's not clearly understood to make an instant decision.

The fire drill escalates next to a conference call with the vendor where the dealer's reports are supplemented with additional data. The vendor attempts to make the case for the value of their product. In some cases, the additional data reveals that a product is just not working, and the product is cancelled.

Isn't it interesting, that in order for dealers to understand the ROI of vendor services, this level of escalation is needed?

Dealers love numbers. They live and die by numbers. The pace of change in the automotive retail industry has unfortunately flooded dealers with more data than they can understand and manage. This situation needs a speedy resolution, because business operations aren't getting more data driven.

What's needed is a set of equations that accepts key data points from each vendor's product or service. These equations give the dealership the information needed to manage and make decisions about the product. More important, dealers aren't flooded with data that they don't need for decision-making.

DEALERS DON'T WANT DATA DISTRACTIONS

A perfect example of being flooded by data is Google Analytics. If a dealer wanted to know how their website was performing, it wouldn't be uncommon for them to be directed to print a Google Analytics report. The default report format shows more than 50 performance metrics over the last 30 days.

Included in the standard report are metrics that include bounce rate, unique visitors, time on site, number of page views, referral traffic, goals, mobile visitors, exit pages, entry pages, etc.

Handing a standard Google Analytics report to the dealer principal or general manager could be a waste of time. Why? It most likely won't give them the assistance they need to inspect their website investment.

Most likely the standard analytics report will evoke questions like:

- "What should I be looking at on this report?"

- "How does this data compare to other dealers?"

- "How can I see the impact of the $5,000 increase in paid search we made last month?"

- Did adding chat change our website traffic patterns or time on site?

What the dealer needs to see is the relationship between the investments that drive website traffic to desired outcomes, which can include calls, leads, appointments, and sales. The 50-plus metrics provided in Google Analytics aren't what a dealer principal needs to review. What they need is a summary of what's important to their dealership.

Dealers will want to know if their vendor metrics compare well to similar dealers in their market that use the same technology platform. Most vendor reports need a translator, so get one.

ENTER THE EXECUTIVE DASHBOARD

As you're reading this, don't focus on how the data inputs are collected. Some data elements can be automated, and some will be input from the back office. What we can't continue to repeat is printing reports that aren't useful for making actual business decisions.

Wouldn't it be great to combine the report data from all your vendors in one place? Have the monthly results, charts and trends from your business equations on one dashboard. This would make it convenient for executives to inspect and act on the data presented every month.

This isn't a fantasy, and it's what mega dealer groups are doing to create a competitive edge over stand-alone stores and smaller groups. They have the resources and MBA graduates pumping data into spreadsheets to find the leaks in the budget and marketing strategy.

There are two paths that dealers can take to creating an Executive Dashboard (ED). They can create a tool using open-source products like Microsoft Excel, or they can purchase a third-party tool to accomplish an automated display of data and reports.

In the first case, using Excel is a quick and easy way to set up a template that can be manually filled in each month to create summary reports for the executive team. The challenge is to understand which metrics from each vendor really are important and how the data relates to other products and services.

I personally work with dealers to create Excel templates that are customized for their dealership. Spreadsheets can also grow over time allowing dealers to start with some basics and build out a more complex tool. Spreadsheets are extremely powerful and bring the insights and alerts that larger corporations have had at their disposal for years.

The second option is to purchase an online tool designed to allow easy input of dealership data and provide the consolidated reporting and analysis needed for executive decisions. I've been developing such a dashboard reporting tool for my clients for more than two years. I'll offer all dealers reading this book an opportunity to receive a free trial of the product.

By visiting this website www.roi-bot.com, dealers can register for a free trial by using offer code UFA69. This will give dealers time to input data and see the power behind creating an ED for their vendor partners providing data feeds for their products.

Dealers seeking an Unfair Advantage to stay ahead of their competition need to run their businesses using data and analytics. They need to use an ED built to make data-based, not emotional-based decisions. The decision dealers have to make is whether they'll build it themselves in Excel or purchase a customized online tool.

DASHBOARDS CAN ASSIST WITH BILLING AUDITS

A dealer recently showed me a vendor report documenting their monthly costs for Google Adwords management. In the report, the numbers of "clicks" were shown for each keyword, with a total at the bottom representing clicks for the month. Those clicks from the vendor's Google Adwords report *should match* the pay-per-click (PPC) traffic counts displayed in Google Analytics.

If the dealer's spreadsheet had input fields for monthly Adwords' clicks from their vendor partner and another field for Google Analytics Adwords' clicks, a formula could be created to show the difference, if any.

If the difference were large, the spreadsheet would clearly alert the dealer, because the font in the spreadsheet cell could turn red. The red text would indicate that something isn't correct with billing. Knowing how to relate these data points just created something useful for the dealership—a simple audit for PPC investments. Without such a tool, I'm not confident that the dealer would have compared these two data points manually.

DASHBOARDS CAN ASSIST WITH STRATEGY

Dealers are always seeking insight into the ROI of their digital marketing and traditional media vendors. With an ED, dealers can input their monthly costs and report data for radio, cable TV, newspaper, Google Adwords, Craigslist, SEO or other advertising partners.

When the ED is integrated with Google Analytics data, a number of insights can be instantly seen. For one dealer, their ED showed that their Google Adwords campaign was eight times more effective than their combined radio and newspaper investments to drive qualified traffic to their website. Increasing qualified traffic was one of the goals this dealer wanted to see on their dashboard.

DASHBOARDS CAN SHOW IMBALANCES

In the book *Winning the Zero Moment of Truth*, author Jim Lecinski introduces the term Zero Moment of Truth (ZMOT), along with previously defined industry terms like First Moment of Truth (FMOT) and Second Moment of Truth (SMOT). Research shared by Lecinski showed that consumer-purchasing decisions were influenced by Stimulus, ZMOT and FMOT. How their vehicles performed and how they were treated after the sale greatly influenced SMOT.

Investments in retention and loyalty (SMOT) are also very important; when a consumer first buys a car, they're 100 percent loyal. What we do after that moment determines how fast that loyalty will drop.

When dealers input their marketing and operations investments on a monthly basis, it's very common to see a large portion of the budget going to Stimulus spending. Much too often the funding for FMOT and SMOT investments is too low. Dealers who are over-spending on stimulus aren't maximizing the profit potential of their dealerships.

A well-designed ED can make it easy for dealership executives to see when their budgetary decisions put their marketing strategy out of balance. The budget percentage for Stimulus, ZMOT, FMOT and SMOT needs to be customized for each dealership; there's no one perfect set of percentages. However, once set, the ED that shows the percentages of spending each month can yield some very powerful insights.

GET YOUR VENDOR DATA ORGANIZED

Every dealership is unique and requires the right tools, vendor partners, employees and training to maximize profitability, and to build an excellent reputation in their community. With that said, dealers all face the need to operate their businesses with greater insights into the effectiveness of their operating budgets. It's time to tame the data-reporting monster. Time to get our business goals and data aligned. Time to stop running from the details and embrace the summarized outcomes.

CHAPTER 16

Knowing Your Audience in Fixed Operations

By Jim Bernardi

When I think about the numerous resources that connect customers to dealerships, I can't help wonder if dealers truly know who their audience is? Have they leveraged this audience to create an Unfair Advantage in their market for fixed operations?

The dealer's "audience" is greater than the names that are stored in the Dealership Management System (DMS) database. It is the intersection of the people in the dealer's database and the people who these prior customers influence. It also includes owners of vehicles who are "brand" loyal but have yet to interact with the dealership that sells that same brand.

Dealers who have not done a great job in managing their database have let customers fall through the cracks. Dealers must not focus on past mistakes or missed opportunities. Instead they must focus on handling today's customers properly. If a dealer's fixed operations CSI scores in the past have been low, there is no barrier to starting fresh with every service customer who arrives today. If the dealer's CSI scores have led their region, then it will be easier to leverage the advice in this chapter.

A powerful stream of revenue is standing in dealer showrooms right now. Putting customers first every time will not only increase gross profit margins, it will influence the marketplace! Happy customers will likely share their experience with friends or neighbors and may also share their experience online. If that experience is bad, then the amplification can be even greater due to the power of online review websites like Google Places, Yelp.com, or DealerRater.com

KNOWING YOUR AUDIENCE

Customer satisfaction exists at the intersection of expectations, processes and staff performance. Here are the top six reasons why customers stop coming to a dealership:

1. Were treated with an attitude of indifference by the dealer and/ or an employee (68 percent)

2. Are dissatisfied with the product (14 percent)

3. Go to your competition (9 percent)

4. Develop other friendships, both professionally and personally (5 percent)

5. Move away (3 percent)

6. Die (1 percent)

Feedback from the dealer's audience is instrumental in understanding the factors that impact the flow of new work. Dealers that want to accelerate their fixed-operations profits must get an accurate survey from current customers.

Without a "standard" at the dealership team, it is nearly impossible to have any expectations for employees to achieve excellence. Employees must completely understand the standard set by the dealership. Dealers should also provide enough feedback and tracking tools that will allow employees to see the dealership standard as part of their job descriptions. It should be clear to employees that no deviations from this standard will be accepted.

ARE DEALERS COMMITTED TO CHANGE?

Let's change lanes here for a moment. I really love historical stories and facts, so allow me to illustrate a great historical story that I find very relevant to management at dealerships:

In 1519, the Spanish explorer Cortez sailed his fleet of 11 ships into the harbor of Vera Cruz, Mexico. It was common practice in those days to leave guards with the ships, as they might be needed to later return to the Old World for supplies or, if necessary, to retreat from the enemy. But Cortez came for victory; he did not come to look at "options." He didn't want anyone to have any doubts about their mission, so he gave the order to "burn the ships." Obviously, Cortez wasn't ambivalent about victory. Nothing short of victory was acceptable!

When Cortez gave his orders to burn the ships, his men no doubt "got it" that he was serious about this mission. It takes commitment like this if you really want results. But in today's world, what's a typical commitment by most people? All too often it's a lukewarm response that says, "Sure I can give it a shot," and with one hand outstretched, we reach for the stars. But just in case things don't work out, we keep our other hand firmly grasped to the chair in our familiar and comfortable office in the world of the known and predictable. As I read somewhere: When the going gets tough, those who keep one eye on the way out usually loses.

We all go through times in our lives when we know we must commit to change, and in some cases, significant change. If we are honest, we will admit change scares the daylights out of us. We all want the potential reward and excitement that change offers, and there's often real excitement in our voice when we *talk* about the challenge. But talk is cheap. Commitment requires real action; the kind of action Cortez took when he gave to order, "Burn the ships."

Fully committing to success means there are no excuses. If dealership employees commit to increasing sales, then they burn the ship of excuses because nothing short of total realization of that goal is acceptable. Old sales goals are gone forever, and the only things they are focused on are the new numbers. Falling back and hitting the old numbers isn't a success of any kind; it's short of the goal.

If a person commits to meeting with one new client every week, and previously met with one new client every three months, burn that ship of *what used to be acceptable*. It's gone! Meet the goal established!

Simply saying "I want to do this or that" isn't good enough. Commitment requires that we change the verb from *want* to *will*. I *will* contact new prospects this week, I *will* make this deadline, and I *will* change my attitude.

Burn the ship of options and excuses and make a real commitment! No more "woulda," "coulda" or "shoulda," and no mindset of "I will go down fighting." I will not go down fighting, because I will not fail!

If you want to win, don't allow losing to be an option. Victory comes with the commitment that is willing to "burn the ships."

I'm not stating that dealers burn the proverbial ship; I am merely suggesting that they make it a company policy to fight the good fight and never give in to negative employee relations that certainly slows the tides of progression. Dealers must ensure that their team is committed to go the distance. They must demand perfection in all they accomplish each and every day. Consumers are certainly expecting a bigger bang for their buck.

> Your Action: When you make your next commitment, write it down on a piece of paper and keep it in a conspicuous place where you will see it daily. Begin with "I will," not "I want."

CUSTOMER SATISFACTION FOUNDATIONS

Customer service is an integral part of automotive retaking and should not be seen as an extension of it. A dealer's most vital asset is their customer. Without customers, dealerships would not and could not exist.

The practice of customer service should be as present on the showroom floor as it is in any other sales environment and/or department. Every department *is the showroom floor*!

1. **Remember who the boss is.** We are in business to service *customer needs*, and we can only do that if we know what our customers want. When we truly listen to our customers, they let us know what they want. Never forget that the customer pays our salary and makes our jobs possible.

2. **Be a good listener.** Take the time to identify customer needs by asking questions and concentrating on what the customer

is really saying. Listen to their words, tone of voice, body language, and most important, how they feel. Beware of making assumptions, thinking you intuitively know what the customer wants. There is a great danger of preoccupation when you're looking around to see to who else you could be selling, especially if your lead or customer seems to be going awry. Stay focused!

3. *Identify and anticipate needs.* Customers don't buy products or services. They buy good feelings and solutions to problems. Most sales purchases are based on emotional rather than logical needs. The more we know our customers, the better we become at anticipating their needs. Communicate regularly so you are aware of problems or upcoming needs or concerns.

4. *Make customers feel important and appreciated.* Treat them as individuals. Always use their name and find ways to compliment them, but be sincere. People value sincerity. It creates good feelings and trust. Think about ways to generate good feelings about doing business with you. Customers know whether or not you really care about them, so thank them every time you get a chance.

5. *Be sure that your body language conveys sincerity on the showroom floor or service department.* Your words and actions should be congruent.

6. *Help customers understand the dealership's processes.* A dealer may have the best processes, but if customers don't understand them, they can get confused, impatient and angry. Employees must take time to explain how the dealership works and how transactions are completed. Be careful that the explanation does not sound mechanical and robotic.

7. *Appreciate the power of "Yes."* Always look for ways to help your customers. When they have a request (as long as it is reasonable), tell them that you can do it. Figure out how afterward. Look for ways to make doing business with you easy.

8. ***Know how to apologize and when.*** When something goes wrong, apologize. It's easy and customers like it. The customer may not always be right, but the customer must always win. Deal with problems immediately and let customers know what will be done to resolve the matter. Make it simple for customers to complain. Value their complaints or concerns and have a solution built into the equation for solving it in a timely manner. Even if customers are having a bad day, dealers should go out of their way to make them feel comfortable.

9. ***Give more than expected.*** Since the future of all companies lies in keeping customers happy, think of ways to elevate the dealership above the competition. Consider the following:

   a. What can the dealership give customers that they cannot get elsewhere?

   b. What can the dealership do to follow up and thank people even when they don't buy?

   c. What can the dealership give customers that is totally unexpected?

10. ***Get regular feedback.*** Encourage and welcome suggestions about how the dealership can improve. There are several ways in which dealers can find out what customers think and feel about their services.

    a. Listen carefully to what they say.

    b. Check back regularly to see how things are going.

    c. Provide a method that invites constructive criticism, comments and suggestions.

11. ***Treat your staff/employees well.*** Employees are internal customers and need a regular dose of appreciation. Thank them and find ways to let them know how important they are. Treat employees with respect, and chances are they will have a higher regard for customers. Appreciation stems from the top. Treating customers and employees well is equally important.

LEAD NURTURING IN THE SERVICE DEPARTMENT

Lead nurturing is a system that allows the dealer to send an automated series of emails to an early-stage lead in order to prequalify them. While lead nurturing is inherently a sales tool, it can also be used as a customer-lead nurturing tool. That is, it can be used to:

- Create loyalty

- Build top of mind

- Influence referrals

- Reach orphan owners

Customer nurturing is a special type of email series that moves the customer down the funnel from just obtaining service to coming back to the service department when the need arises, such as with an oil change. Since the customer-nurturing series is automated it happens in the background without any interactions from the service advisor. This limits the "oh, I forgot to follow up" mentality that some service advisors have.

One of the biggest pluses of a nurturing program is that a promotional email will receive 4 to 10 times the amount of response of a normal email blast. Email blasts work but only with a small number of people.

- **Sample email blast:** 5,000 emails with a 7 percent open rate and a 3 percent click-through rate = 10 people seeing your promotion

- **Email as part of a customer-nurturing campaign:** 5,000 emails with a 20 percent open rate and an 8 percent click-through rate = 80 people seeing your promotion

With an average of 1 percent of people clicking through from an email blast accepting the offer (such as a coupon for an oil change), you can expect one sale from blasting an email out to 5,000 people. During a customer-nurturing campaign, an average of 12.5 percent of people will accept the offer, resulting in 10 sales from the same 5,000 people. If you have an average upsell of $70 per RO, then it's the difference between $70 and $700.

5 Steps to Setting Up a Customer-Nurturing Campaign

1. What problem are you going to help them solve?

   - Maintenance issues?

   - DIY jobs?

2. Which content are you going to share?

3. Set up a timeline.

4. Get customer to agree to receive info.

5. Measure and improve.

   - Open rate

   - Click-through rate

   - Conversion rate

   - Unsubscribe rate (less than 1 percent)

Example Lead-Nurturing Campaign

- *Email day 1:* Thank you for choosing us. (link to post about routine maintenance)

- *Email Day 7:* "15 Things You Need to Know to Keep Your Vehicle Out of the Shop" (link to post)

- *Email Day 21:* What can we do better to serve you? (survey)

- *Email Day 42:* Social proof (refer-a-friend incentive)

- *Email Day 65:* Link to post about the importance of the oil change along with a coupon.

- *Email Day 90:* "5 Things You Can Do Yourself and Save a Trip to the Service Department" (link to post)

With this example, we are creating a loop from one oil change to the next by educating the customer, then offering them a coupon before the need for an oil change arises. Also, we take the time to ask their opinion on how our service is. This serves as a way for them to vent if they need to and gives us an opportunity to fix it and re-earn their business.

Optimizing Your Customer-Nurturing Campaign
• Keep the email short and to the point.

    o Link to blog for more info.

• Keep it personal.

    o Use customer's first name.

    o Send from real email.

    o Be authentic.

• Don't send too many; spread them out.

• Create a signature with links to your social networks.

• Stay on topic.

• Create multiple campaigns.

• Include a call to action.

• Write subject lines that get opened.

    o First line(s) need to be very compelling.

I hope this lesson was able to help you understand your fixed operations in a different light and provide you and your staff an Unfair Advantage over your competition.

About Jim

Jim Bernardi has been recognized as "The Consummate Fixed Operations Expert by Automotive Executives Worldwide." He has more than 35 years of experience in fixed operations recruiting, training, management and marketing. He has been a contributing author in several automotive magazines for many years and is the Founder and Publisher of Automotive Dealers Network.

Jim continues to travel the globe educating dealers and manufacturers on the importance of sales in fixed-operations management for his training company: AutoPro Training Solutions. When he is not training a dealer group or a dealership, you will find him as a guest speaker at many dealer 20 Group meetings.

He offers real-world solutions to dealers and manufacturers in more than 49 countries worldwide. He is always looking to better serve the franchised automotive world. He continues to offer a three-day comprehensive fixed-operations performance review to dealers nationwide and performs these reviews personally.

CHAPTER 17

What You Should Know About Auto Dealer Chat to Gain the Advantage

By Shereef Moawad

Auto dealer chat is growing fast and expected to double in 2012 from approximately 20 percent to 40 percent, and is forecast to be on 70 percent of dealers websites by the end of 2013. Early adaptors that have effectively managed chat and are using good, proactive chat software have a huge advantage over their competitors. They are interacting and promoting their dealership website. They are establishing a rapport with their website visitors instead of letting them browse the site in hopes they might submit a contact request. Would you just let people wander around on your dealership lot in hopes that they might come inside and ask to be assisted? Of course not.

Dealers with effectively managed chat are gaining up to a 100 percent increase in leads from their websites. Where are these leads coming from? Their competition! Instead of just letting potential customers fill out a website contact form or call in from someone else's website, they engage them in a chat conversation and start a relationship, which results in the customer giving up their contact information, and possibly even setting an appointment to come into the dealership.

A dealer's website is their best possible source for new customer acquisition. These site visitors more than likely have already heard of your dealership and are considering doing business with you. Why else would they be there! They want to buy a car, get their car serviced or purchase parts.

Every dime you spend on marketing and promotion is inevitably pushing more traffic to your dealership website. Why spend thousands more on marketing, pay per click, and other internet campaigns to gain only 3 percent to 5 percent as leads? This doesn't sound like the smartest path when you can increase conversion for a lot less money from your current traffic. The thousands of visitors you already have are the ones that will convert better and close at a higher rate. Doesn't it make sense to maximize the lead conversion from your best source?

At this point you're likely thinking, "I'll just add auto dealer chat software to my site, and we will be all set! I'm sure we can get some staff in sales or our BDC to add this to whatever they are doing." Not quite. Just like anything else worthwhile, to use dealer chat effectively takes research and understanding. Processes need to be developed and 100 percent of your chat queries need to be answered. You wouldn't just let your phone ring off the hook with no answer at your dealership, would you? If chats are missed, then you are better off without it on your website, as you will alienate your website visitors instead of increasing your odds of selling them.

You also need good, proactive chat software with strong reporting so you can see your strengths and weaknesses. Here is your shopping list if you want to manage chat in-house:

1. Find good, proactive auto dealer-specific chat software.

2. Decide who is going to take the chats.

3. Decide who is going to manage the process.

4. Develop effective scripts to start with that will help you achieve your goals.

5. Develop your policies and procedures and best practices for all chat types (sales new, sales used, service requests and part's requests).

6. Train your chat staff on the policies and procedures, scripts and best practices.

Now it's time to execute and learn/improve as you go. In order to expect good results, you need to effectively manage the process. If any of the above six items on the shopping list are not done effectively or skipped, then your results will not be as strong as they could be.

There is more bad news, but it can be avoided. A large percentage of dealers that attempt to manage chat in-house do not get good results and fail. The reason they fail is because they don't have a solid plan of action, a good process, a solid understanding of chat, or effective chat management.

I will address some major areas that cause dealers to fail, which may seem simple, but unfortunately, don't seem to be understood.

- Using non-proactive chat yields a very small amount of chat conversations. If you don't greet visitors, you are missing the boat (you greet your dealership visitors, don't you?). Proactive chat increases interaction by 75 to 80 percent, and will give you a lot more opportunities to gain info or an appointment.

- If you require chat visitors to enter their contact info before they can chat with you (name, email, phone), then the amount of interaction will be greatly reduced. What makes chat appealing to site visitors is they can be anonymous until they decide not to be. When chat is set up to require info first, it is doomed to fail.

- You have to answer the chat! NADA studies show that dealers managing their own chats miss 55 percent of chat requests during business hours. As I mentioned before don't attempt to add in-house managed chat if you cannot ensure that all requests are answered.

- A solid plan of action and great chat scripts are needed. If you think being nice and giving all the info requested will gain you conversion, then you need to think about what traditionally happens to a car salesman in their first and second month. The first month they only have the info they have been trained under and don't know all the answers, but sell a bunch of cars. The second month they normally experience a large drop in sales. If you've been in the business a while, then you know why. They now know a lot more information and are happy to share it

171

freely. They make friends, not sales. In the first month when they were asked something they didn't know, they moved forward with the process, told the client they were new and would do their best to find the answers to all their questions, then kept on selling. I know I am beating this to death, but the point is you are not there engaging in chats just to make friends and give information. You are there to gain leads you can follow up on and set appointments to sell cars, service and parts.

Another big reason for failure is when salespeople from the floor are asked to monitor their computer or mobile device to take chats. The problem is that about 50 to 60 percent of chat requests are not vehicle-sales related. How many parts and service chats do you think it will take to severely black out your salesman? How well do you think they will interact with your service and parts prospects? I think it is obvious what the answers are, but sometimes managers seem to forget those salespeople are commission based. One way to address this issue would be to only place chat on your vehicle sales pages, but not all sales-related site visitors will make it to those pages; many leave from the home page, so this would not be maximizing the opportunity.

To maximize chat, you need staff available from all three major departments so chats can be routed to the correct department. This takes time effort, effective planning and investment. Some smaller dealers and even larger dealers that are currently maximizing the use of all support, management, and sales staffs' time would need to add dedicated staff and would not realize as strong of a return on investment. For many dealers, it would be more cost effective and offer a much better return on investment to hire a reasonably priced professional auto dealer chat support service.

The good news is there are some great companies that offer auto dealer-specific chat support services and software. These services start at around $295 monthly for the average size dealership, depending on whether it's full service, after-hour's service, proactive or non-proactive, and the traffic your website receives. Some dealer chat companies offer service 24/7 to insure you don't miss any opportunities. When you look at managed staffed support services by the hour they are very inexpensive. A 24/7 service that provides approximately 730 hours support monthly would only be 41 cents an hour based on paying $295 a month.

The best services only deal with car dealerships and have developed effective processes specifically for the car business. The very best dealer chat support companies are run, managed, or heavily consulted by car guys and gals. Even some of the larger software providers, after seeing a large percentage of self-managed failures, are attempting to now offer full-service and after-hours service to improve client retention.

Great proactive auto dealer chat software is just software without great people staffing and managing it. The dealer chat companies that offer managed service focus on one thing alone: auto dealership website chat support. They deal with hundreds of dealerships and often gain a much better result than dealers managing it in-house.

The market is becoming more competitive as more providers enter into the dealer chat support business. If you decide to hire a service, don't be sold by all the bells and whistles of the chat software alone. Most chat providers offer good software, and some do a better job marketing the features and benefits of the software without getting into their results.

It's best to view hiring a dealer chat support provider the same way you do hiring a strong salesman. Look at their past results and talk to their past employers. The best indicator of future performance is past performance, so look at their measurable results as compared to what they charge for their services. Look for third-party feedback on sites like drivingsales.com, or get a list of references to call. You can also view auto dealer chat case study results on the popular automotive dealer forum dealerrefresh.com.

Below are some of the results from the second dealer chat case study my company hosted on Dealer Refresh. These results were posted by volunteer dealers and show two months without and two months with 24/7 staffed dealer chat support services.

AUTO DEALER CHAT CASE STUDY

- Two previous months *without* 24/7 staffed chat support (all three dealers, total of six months combined data before chat):
  Total unique visitors: 27,923
  Web leads: 569
  Website conversion: 2.038 percent

• Two months *with* 24/7 staffed chat support (all 3 dealers, total
 of six months combined data with chat):
 Total unique visitors: 25,035
 Total website leads without chat leads: 545
 Lead conversion percentage without chat leads: 2.176 percent
 Total car chat 24 leads/appointments/queries: 404
 Total conversion percentage with chat leads: 3.79 percent
 Total lead conversion percentage increase: 74.12 percent

Combining all six months' worth of data provided from our three case
study participants shows everything clearly. The numbers speak for
themselves. There was not a drop in website conversion after adding
our 24/7 staffed chat service and an increase in leads of 74 percent with
chat!

Currently the dealers that have effectively added self-managed chat or
are using professional auto dealer-specific chat services are gaining a
huge advantage. Within the next few years it will be on most dealer
sites, and it will be the best software, process, and people combined that
gain the best advantage. Why wait to get on board with auto dealer chat?
The faster you get moving, the sooner you gain the advantage over your
competitors.

About Shereef

When it comes to combining the cutting-edge marketing techniques of today's technology with high-level car sales expertise, few have been as successful as Shereef Moawad, owner of CarChat24.com and ChatLead.com.

After serving America in the U.S. Marine Corps, Shereef took a few business and computer courses at St. Petersburg College, then decided to get the rest of his education where it counted—in the business world. After successful stints at Ford and Nissan dealerships, where he won high honors for his sales management abilities, Shereef ran his own car broker and dealer consulting business, where he assisted auto businesses in creating and optimizing their initial online sales systems. Because of his experience and expertise, he was offered general sales manager position at a Mercedes-Benz dealership, where he created their business development center and also tripled their sales numbers.

From there, he went to work as general sales manager at Ferman BMW/Mini, where he also spurred astonishing sales growth with his innovative technology initiatives. Among his profitable advances at Ferman: developing a BDC to effectively manage incoming queries for sales and service, using other online sites such as eBay to take advantage of consumers' increasing usage of the internet, adding live chat support to Ferman websites to increase leads and provide 24/7 customer service, applying SEO techniques to increase website traffic, managing new and used inventories, and developing and implementing a daily sales training plan to improve sales processes and product knowledge. The results of his efforts was an increase in pre-owned sales by 105 percent, new sales by 45 percent, and an overall increased front-and-back gross profit annually of 52 percent—all of which culminated in the dealership being awarded BMW's highest honor of Center of Excellence.

In 2009, Shereef again went out on his own to work full time on CarChat24.com, the side business he had founded with his wife three years earlier and had grown so fast that it required 100 percent of his attention. CarChat24.com is designed to help dealers sell more vehicles by converting more website visitors into quality leads. Using the most up-to-date live chat software and a proven proactive chat process, CarChat24.com's car dealer clients have seen online sales improve markedly with Shereef's service. CarChat24's success has led Shereef to create a similar service, Chatware.com, to provide software and service support for *any* business vertical.

Shereef has two children: Jessica, 23 and Max, 19. He and his wife, Patricia, who continue to innovate in the field of internet and automotive process building, attend

Calvary Baptist Church in Clearwater, Florida. They enjoy boating, spending family time together, and, of course, cars. Shereef is also a member of the Automotive Dealers Network, Automotive Industry Professionals, the Automotive Website Marketing Group, Dealer Elite, Digital Car Dealers, the Interactive and Digital Media Group, Internet Sales Pros, Christian Professionals Worldwide, and the Semper Fi Network for U.S. Marine Corps Veterans.

CHAPTER 18

Internet/BDC Processes to Avoid Being an Idiot

By Marc McGurren

What do you call it? Is it an internet department, business development center (BDC), internet store, hybrid, customer care team, or loyalty department? No matter the label, all dealers have a team to manage opportunities that come to the store. For automotive retailers, a majority of those opportunities (phone calls, website leads, and showroom ups) are generated from the internet.

The internet is not just a "necessary evil." It's a necessity for car dealers to conduct business. Whether dealers know it or not, every dealership across the country has one of the largest profit makers, or profit leaks in their dealerships—their digital marketing department.

Dealers can no longer ignore the fact that more than 85 percent of their customers are now touching the internet in some way, shape or form before purchasing a vehicle. Most dealers are actively engaged with the internet, but many are not sure they have the processes implemented to maximize the profits the internet offers.

Digital marketing efforts can no longer be farmed out to the young kid who knows how to use social media tools or is considered a geek. Dealers must take a hard look at all their digital processes and communications. Dealers must inspect the messages that are being presented to in-market consumers on behalf of the dealership.

Dealership executives I speak with want clear direction for improving their email processes, phone communications, and marketing strategies to better connect with their leads and retain their customers. In essence, dealers want to know how to operate their BDC/internet department as efficiently and effectively as possible.

Online shoppers have developed "bullshit radar"; they can recognize insincere communications, email auto responders, and evasive tactics that don't answer their questions the first time. Dealers must get back to the basics in their communication strategies.

Digital marketing departments must be real, genuine and authentic. They must embrace building relations with online shoppers. Dealers have to stop taking the easy way out by relying on automated processes that fire out canned emails with no personal touch.

Please don't misunderstand me. I believe strongly in developing processes, phone scripts and email communication templates. What I'm saying is that dealers must get back to personal touches based on a commitment to take better care of the consumers who contact them. This attention to detail will increase contact rates, appointments and car sales. Automated emails work poorly and customers can recognize them from a mile away. It's no wonder why dealers have such a hard time getting a customer on the phone after they've submitted a lead on their website.

I will share BDC/internet strategies that work and deliver outstanding results. These strategies work for high-line, domestic, foreign or independent dealers. The strategies apply basic principles that work for dealers regardless of whether communications with customers are online or on the showroom floor.

When I work with dealers, they'll almost always hear me state passionately, "You cannot fix what you do not know." The first order of business for any internet department or BDC is to figure out exactly how well (or poorly) the department is performing.

Some dealers are frustrated on how to inspect and compare the performance of their internet department. This chapter will give dealers the foundational knowledge that will give them an Unfair Advantage for both sales and fixed operations against competitors in their market.

To create an Unfair Advantage in an internet department/BDC, the steps are not difficult. Dealers should not focus on the perceived "difficulty" of tools like CRM systems or how to set up workflow processes. Proper training will resolve those issues.

THE FIRST ORDER OF BUSINESS: DON'T BE AN IDIOT!

No joke. I challenge all dealership executives to review what digital content is sent out to potential customers each day. Dealers should submit a website lead using a fictitious name and address and even invest in a throw away phone to use on the lead form. When submitting the lead, ask a specific question in the comments box. Dealers may be appalled at what they find from such an audit.

A dealership executive doesn't have to be an "internet person" to conduct an audit. They're an actual consumer who knows how to read and see if the response received matches the specific question they asked on their lead submission. Internet responses are not the only communications that need editorial review.

Someone in the dealership needs to overlook the layout and spelling for an email blast for the big "Persident's Day Sale" (true story), before your President's Day weekend comes around. Think about the impression made on consumers when dealer emails are run-on sentences lacking punctuation and a good spell check!

I have read countless emails where the dealer's departments have consistently made these types of mistakes and have looked like idiots. Are they idiots? Of course not, but they sure can look like one if they are not careful.

I want to encourage dealers to set up a process that has at least two levels of proofreading before any large email blast goes out. All email templates and communication guides should be checked for grammar, spelling and punctuation. Is this important? More than 35 percent of emails I receive when I mystery shop are poorly formatted, contain spelling errors, or contain hyperlinks that are broken.

SECOND ORDER OF BUSINESS: PAY ATTENTION

Now that dealers know they're not looking like idiots to online consumers, it's important for them to pay attention. Remember, *dealers cannot fix what they do not know.* Therefore, dealers must ask themselves relevant questions:

- How is my internet/BDC department performing?
- Is my team overwhelmed?
- Are the team members underwhelming?

Most of this information can be retrieved via the dealer's CRM software.

Here is a list of data points that dealers must collect to build an initial reporting system, which will help them inspect their department. The data is presented in three sections, and the details should be expanded/customized for each dealership:

Leads and Sales:
- How many leads are coming in? (phones and digital)
- How many appointments are being set from those opportunities?
- How many appointments are showing from the appointments set?
- How many cars were sold?

Lead Sources:
- How many opportunities were received from each lead provider?
- How many appointments and shows per lead provider?
- How much does each lead provider cost?
- What is the average cost per lead?
- What is the average cost per sale?
- How much gross profit (both front and back) is being made per sale per lead provider?

Salespeople/BD Agents:
- How many leads is each agent receiving?
- How many appointments, appointment shows, and sold?

These lists of just the start of paying attention to the data that can help dealers audit their department's performance. Once dealers know how they are performing, they can make the decisions or ask questions on how to improve performance.

THIRD ORDER OF BUSINESS: STRUCTURE

Now that dealers have learned how not to be an idiot, and have decided to pay attention, it's now time to start giving their department some structure.

There is not one perfect model for running a "digital marketing" department. I know dealers that have a "cradle to grave" process that is successful. I also know of dealers that swear by their BDC department that only sets appointments. There are pros and cons to all process styles, but it comes down to what works best for the individual dealership.

With that said, my personal opinion of the best way to have an Unfair Advantage in today's market is through an *efficiently run* BDC. Many dealerships do not have an efficient BDC and, therefore, what is supposed to be a profit maker has turned out to be a profit leak.

So how do any dealers set up their department? It would be impossible to spell out how to set up a BDC or internet department in one chapter. What I will say is that regardless of how any dealer sets up their departmental structure, it starts with one person.

Often dealers do not have the time, energy and knowledge to build an efficient BDC, but I would guarantee that someone in their dealership or an industry consultant has the answers. It's not necessarily the twenty-something "kid" who knows a little about computers and nothing about sales. All it takes is someone to catch the vision, after being properly trained and coached. Add a heavy dose of passion to that employee, and any dealer can be on the right path to creating an Unfair Advantage in their marketplace.

Once a dealer finds that "someone," now what? Passion without training is like trying to ride an unbroken, unbridled horse. Possible? Yes. Sustainable? No way.

Dealers should discuss with their peers the best conferences, workshops and trainers that can help to educate their team. Invaluable information is also provided on industry blogs and digital marketing communities. For a list of recommended online resources, visit www.unfairadvantagebooks.com.

If a dealer is starting or rebuilding their internet team, they can avoid blunders and expedite success by hiring a consultant/trainer. In full disclosure, that's exactly what I do for a living, and there are a number of great consultants in our industry that dealers can choose from. Having the right coach will help get dealerships pointed in the right direction quickly.

I recommend a five-tiered approach to setting up a BDC. Each tier can be implemented one by one as staff, comfort level and training are in the proper place.

1. Digital leads

2. Finance and equity database mining

3. Fixed operations

4. Unsold showroom follow-up

5. Sold and CSI follow-up

Where should a dealer start? I recommend starting with the greatest opportunity. Many times this is the way digital leads are handled and/or fixed operations. Depending on staffing, any of these can be started when a dealer is ready to flip the BDC switch.

Digital lead management can be tricky without a knowledgeable captain driving the digital ship. This is often the greatest need in a dealership. So what's a dealer to do? Keep the ship moving forward and inspect everything until the right leadership is in place!

Any dealer knows that fixed operations can be one of the most profitable arms of the business and therefore needs to be of the upmost importance inside the dealership. A fixed operations-centered BDC can take incoming phone calls, set first appointments, drive retention, call back declined service, and much more.

Lastly, but certainly not least, a dealer must follow up with their current sold database and make sure their customer is beyond satisfied with the experience at the dealership. Most dealers already have something in place like this but it isn't necessarily a BDC. Regardless of who's calling and following up, this *must* be done well in any dealership.

Any dealership can implement these tiers at any given time, and they can be rolled out according to their comfort level and training. A decision not to implement is a decision in it of itself. Indecisiveness cannot and should not be acceptable.

OK Marc, I'm moving forward with some or all of these tiers. Now what?

THE FOURTH ORDER OF BUSINESS: PROCESS

Process is where the automotive retail industry struggles the most. Dealers today make the investment to have a decent website, and many are dabbling in some form of digital advertising. But what happens once the customer contacts the dealership?

Every market and franchise is different, but best practices can assist any dealership. I've created an outline to gauge a dealership's process in the following graphic:

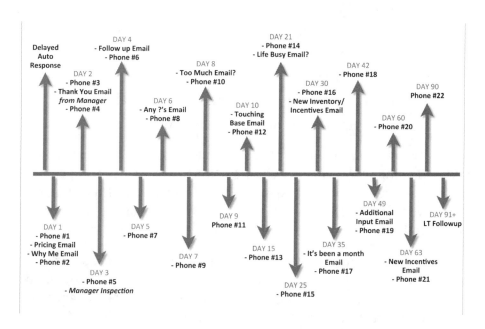

This chart is customized for every dealership I consult with. The theme: being pleasantly persistent. Dealerships were spamming before we had a "spam folder" in our inbox. In the past, dealers have been known to be annoying, overbearing, and an utter nuisance, hence why most customers do not want to deal with car dealers.

Once a customer submits a lead, I am a firm believer in connecting with the person on the phone prior to sending out a price quote. I believe in pricing a customer every time. The reason for connecting with the consumer over the phone first? To "sell" the representative and the dealership!

Customers still buy cars from people and want to deal with a real person. If the dealer can "sell" themselves and the dealership prior to the competition, the chance of earning the customer's trust exponentially increases, and so does selling a vehicle.

If the internet/BDC representative connects with a voice mail rather than a live person, leave a message. The representative should leave the following:

- Their name
- The name of the dealership
- Repeat what the customer was looking for based on the submitted form
- Answers to any questions they had
- A reminder to check their spam filter for their email
- The dealership's phone number, repeated twice

A dealership sets the stage by stating what information was received and then what the representative will be sending over. Once the voice mail is left, send a *personal* price quote over immediately. A dealership does not have to be the cheapest price, but they better be competitive in the marketplace.

I don't care how great a dealership is, if they're $1,000 to $2,000 higher than anyone on the block, it's hard to overcome. Therefore, dealers must be students of their market by regularly mystery shopping their competition to make sure they're in the ballpark when it comes to pricing.

The follow-up schedule a dealer uses needs to take on the theme of being pleasantly persistent. Follow up enough to let them know you care but not too much where you are "that dealership." Be personal, and be competitive.

BRINGING IT ALL TOGETHER:
THE FINAL ORDER OF BUSINESS

Once dealers have decided to not be an idiot, are paying attention, have the right structure and process, they must bring it all together to implement and inspect. Starting, changing or tweaking a dealer's digital marketing department can be scary, at times risky, and downright stressful. I can guarantee it will be worth it the investment in time.

A dealer's internet department/BDC could be the biggest profit center or profit leak in a dealership. Shouldn't it have as much respect as any other department? I believe it should, but sadly it does not.

So my challenge to any dealer is to hold up the mirror and look themselves in the eye, and ask if they're doing everything they can to maximize the opportunities the internet delivers. If the answer is no, they must remove those barriers.

Dealers must be bold, strong and decisive. Will mistakes be made? Undoubtedly. Will profits be realized? Exponentially? Undoubtedly, yes!

About Marc

Marc McGurren joined PCG Consulting Inc. as a partner in January 2012. Formerly he was the Internet Director for the Jerry Durant Auto Group in Weatherford, Texas. He is a graduate of Angelo State University (BBA, 2001), Dallas Theological Seminary (MA/BS, 2003), and the NADA Dealer Candidate Academy (2010). He is currently pursuing his MBA at the University of North Texas.

Most recently, Marc was featured on the cover of *WardsAuto Dealer Business* magazine for his strategies on being one of the top General Motors internet dealerships in the country. He is a regular contributor and former community editor for Drivingsales.com, speaker at multiple automotive conferences, including the Digital Dealer Workshops, Driving Sales Executive Summit, and Digital Marketing Strategies Conference.

With more than seven years of automotive experience, he has held positions ranging from salesperson, sales manager, finance manager, general manager, assistant service and parts director, as well has his current position as internet director. His passion and desire to execute digital marketing strategies is contagious, and his track record of "you can't fix what you don't know" has helped the Jerry Durant Auto Group have the best year in 42 years and sell more than 10,800 cars in 2011.

CHAPTER 19

Online Reviews and Moldy Hotels

By Brian Pasch

One of the many cultural changes brought on by the internet is the reach and influence of peer reviews. When I was growing up, I remember watching Siskel & Ebert with anticipation each week on TV as they reviewed upcoming movies. There are many professional movie critics today that people respect, however, massive change has swept our world in regards to how consumers create and consume reviews.

Consumers have shifted to a peer review model that greatly influences their purchasing, travel, dining, and even career choices. Websites such as TripAdvisor, Yelp, and in the automotive industry, DealerRater were all early pioneers of peer review portals. When Google jumped into the review games with the introduction of Google Places, business owners had no choice but to take notice of the importance of customer reviews.

I was speaking at a 20 Group meeting, and I asked the dealers in attendance, "If you read a review on TripAdvisor for a hotel that stated that its rooms had slightly moldy walls and carpets, would you stay there?" Most dealers said, "no." One dealer chuckled and said, "It depends on the price!" The group erupted in laughter. I wasn't sure if the dealer was joking because his peers added that he was well known to be tight with his money.

Regardless of price, I would not book a hotel with that type of review when so many choices exist. The same applies for car dealers and their reviews. Most dealers have local, same-franchise competition just minutes away from their dealership. Dealers need a way to stand out from their local competitors.

Adding positive reviews on popular websites is one of those strategies that connect with consumers. If negative reviews are found for a dealership without balanced positive commentary, they are akin to the moldy hotel—no one will want to stop in!

Dealers looking for an Unfair Advantage must revise the dealership operations manual to include processes that encourage customers to share their experiences with the dealership online. That communication must start inside the dealership before the customer leaves the showroom or service drive. Dealers cannot afford to allow any customer to leave less than satisfied, because irate customers have great power to influence the next customer in the Zero Moment of Truth, as Jim Lecinski explained in his book, *Winning the Zero Moment of Truth*.

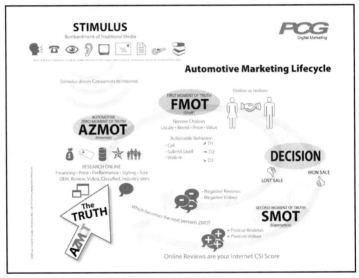

If every customer were asked, "How was your experience at the dealership today?" it would be difficult to miss facial signals and body language that would indicate a potential problem. For the majority of customers, the answer will be positive; for the minority that are less than pleased, it is the dealership's prime opportunity to make things right. I can't urge dealers strongly enough to implement this question in the sales and service processes. Highlight this section if needed; its impact cannot be minimized.

For the customers that respond warmly, it is now the perfect time to shift the discussion toward the power of online reviews. While a customer is inside the dealership, the likelihood that an online review will be posted increases 20 times when compared to asking once the customer leaves the dealership. The subtle point that cannot be missed is how the customer is asked to participate.

Reviews are most effective when they are personalized. An online review that mentions the name of the dealership employee that helped the customer increases the authenticity of the content. Additionally, reviews that mention the car that was purchased or traded gives the review a higher quality because of the level of detailed information provided.

Since dealers want to increase high-quality online reviews, the best results are achieved when they ask their customers face to face. If Gabe sells a car to Jeff, later during the delivery process, Gabe could have a conversation that goes something like this:

Gabe: "Jeff, how was your experience here at Francis Honda?"

Jeff: "It was great."

Gabe: "Did I answer all your questions today?"

Jeff: "Yes, I can't wait to show my family the new car."

Gabe: "Jeff, did you use the internet to research cars?"

Jeff: "Yes. I saw that your dealership had good reviews."

Gabe: "Jeff, reviews are like online referrals. They mean a lot to my success and me. Before you go, could you take a minute to share your excellent experience at Francis Honda online?"

Jeff: "Sure, how do I do that?"

Gabe: "Use this iPad. Do you have a Google Gmail or Yelp account?"

Jeff: "No, I don't have either."

Gabe: "No problem, just complete the online review form on this iPad; It will just take one minute."

There are a few points to note in this hypothetical dialogue. First, the sales professional (Gabe) asked the customer to help him. Gabe asked Jeff to review him personally and not the dealership. The dealership is an "entity"; the experience was provided by Gabe. By asking in this manner, customers are more likely to reciprocate the assistance they just received through purchasing or servicing their vehicle.

Second, the sales professional asked if the customer had a Google or Yelp account first. If the customer responded affirmatively, then they would be directed to click on the Google+ Local icon app or Yelp app on the iPad. The iPad app allows the customer to record their experience inside the dealership. Depending on the local market, other review apps could be added to the iPad.

If the customer did not have a Google or Yelp account, the customer was directed to place a review on an in-store review collection platform. This is an additional piece of software I recommend that dealers purchase. The software allows all customers to share their experience on a dealer-owned review website.

Customized review collection platforms allow customers to post a review in the store as well as from home using the internet. There are no restrictions placed on customers, which allows those who do not have Google or Yelp accounts to post reviews.

The advantages of using a customized reputation management and marketing platform are:

- Custom platforms supplement third-party review websites.
- Dealers can capture reviews from 100 percent of their willing customers.
- Dealers own the reviews and can syndicate the content.
- Review fields can be customized to add more meaningful feedback.
- Photos and/or videos can be added to connect the "text" with an actual person.

Companies that are offering dealers a customized, in-store review collection platform include PrestoReviews.com, BusinessRater.com, and the AutomotiveAdvertisingNetwork.com.

EFFECTIVE THIRD-PARTY REVIEW SITES

Creating a customer review process inside the dealership often triggers dealers to ask which review websites they should be using as part of the online reputation strategy. Unfortunately, there is no single list that applies to all dealers because of regional influences.

New review websites are popping up each month since Yelp went public. Instead of attempting to create a universal list of review websites, I would rather show dealers how to create their own targeted list for their reputation marketing strategies. Since this will be a moving target, readers should check www.UnfairAdvantageBooks.com for the latest list of new review websites that can help dealers with their online reputations.

Before I list specific review websites, it is important to cover some ground rules. Dealers should never post a fake review. They should never take a customer's email praising the dealership and post it as an online review using a fake user account. Dealers should never hire a vendor service that offers to post reviews on their behalf. The downside risks are significant.

Dealers sell and service hundreds of cars every month. From my experience, over 95 percent of dealership customers are happy after a sale or service, so there is no need for dealers to cut corners. Dealers will be surprised just how willing happy customers will be to post an online review. It starts by asking each customer if they had a positive experience that day in the dealership.

Some review websites do not allow reviews to be posted from inside the dealership. They suspect dealers would cheat, so they require the reviews to be posted from the customer's home. These sites check for the IP addresses of the computer where the review comes from. Before dealers post on any review website from inside the dealership, make sure their posting policy allows that practice.

CORE REVIEW WEBSITES

There are a few sites that universally work for dealers:

- Google Places
- Yahoo Local

- Bing Local
- Yelp
- Edmunds
- Cars.com

Since Yahoo and Bing still attract significant local search traffic each month, dealers should also inspect their business listing on Yahoo and Bing Local. These business listings have places for consumers to post reviews. For most dealers, making sure that they have 20 positive reviews on Yahoo and Bing will be all they need to stand out from their peers who will likely have less than 10 reviews posted.

Yelp is included on the list because at the time of writing this chapter, Apple has selected Yelp as the sole source of business reviews that are displayed by Siri. Using an Apple iPhone 4S, when a person speaks to Siri and says "Ford Dealers," the 4S phone will respond by listing local Ford dealers and their "star" counts on Yelp. Yelp also offers dealers an upgraded paid business listing, which dealers are advised to review and see if the benefits compare to the required investment.

Edmunds is included because it often will appear on page-one search results for a search on a dealership's name. Edmunds is also one of the top five automotive portals used by consumers to research cars. With millions of visitors each month, it is prudent that dealers make sure that their Edmunds listing is powerfully positive.

Cars.com is included since many dealers advertise their cars on this website. Reviews on Cars.com can significantly increase the attractiveness of vehicle listing pages, which can yield more calls and lead submissions. If a dealership is not using Cars.com, they can omit that website.

SECONDARY REVIEW WEBSITES

After this list, there are websites that have very strong visibility in search result pages when a consumer searches a dealership name.

- DealerRater.com
- InsiderPages.com
- Judysbook.com
- CitySearch.com

DealerRater.com deserves special mention because it is the "grand daddy" of car dealer review websites. It was the first website to create and deliver high-quality, dealership specific reviews. DealerRater's visibility in search results can be very strong depending on which part of the country a dealer is located. They also offer dealers an opportunity to upgrade their business listing to include dispute resolution and banner advertising on their business profile.

CREATING A CUSTOMIZED LIST FOR THE DEALERSHIP'S PROCESS

So how does a dealer pick which websites to include in their reputation management processes? The review websites that appear on page one or two of search results for a dealer's name are a great place to start. Why? The number-one search phrase that drives traffic to a dealership website is a search on their name. Sites on pages one and two will be the most likely to be found by consumers researching a dealer's reputation.

Inspect all online business directories and review websites to make sure the dealership name, address, website, business categories and phone number are correct. The correct syndication of dealership contact information is very important. If a dealership has been bought or has gone through a name change, the relevance of this action grows even stronger. Schedule an online directory review this week!

On our reader community website, I will post an exhaustive list of online directories that are valuable to synchronize with dealership contact data. Websites come in and out of favor, so it's best to keep that list updated online.

Dealers are advised to have at least 20 positive reviews on the most visible review sites to present a strong, confident message in their market. Dealers should not place all their eggs in one basket; who can predict which websites consumers will use as part of their research. Compelling photos and videos of happy customers should be loaded on all business listing websites, if they are allowed.

After all critical directories and/or review websites have been updated with at least 20 positive reviews, dealers should place their primary focus on the top three most visible review websites in their market along with their dealer-branded review collection platform.

MARKETING GREAT REVIEWS

Once a dealership has developed enough online reviews, they must leverage third-party review websites in their online marketing strategies. Local consumers will trust the opinions of their peers much more than anything the dealer can claim in an advertisement. Marketing positive reviews is a strong strategy that so many dealers miss.

One way to advertise positive reviews is Google's Adwords Express. If a dealer has invested in encouraging customers to post on Google Places, this is a perfect second act. Google Adwords Express allows dealers to create pay-per-click advertisements that feature the current reviews of their customers. The ad format, shown below, is very powerful because it displays the dealerships name, address, phone number, and most important, their reviews.

The results I have seen from advertising dealership online reviews are very encouraging. In their chapter, "Same Is Lame," contributing authors Jimmy Vee and Travis Miller challenge dealers to stand out from their peers. Review marketing is a perfect way to differentiate a dealership by leveraging what the market has publically said about their experience and value.

THE PAY OFF

It goes without saying that dealers should have a corporate culture to deliver outstanding customer service; an experience that creates raving fans and loyal customers. Online reputation marketing transports the customer's personal in-store experience and shares it with an online community.

As important as that may seem, dealers have chosen to ignore or minimally invest in online reviews. The reality for many dealers is that there are so many things on their to-do lists that reputation management gets pushed to the bottom. It's much sexier to focus on generating traffic, phone calls and leads.

But that is the irony of the situation. Great online reviews increase calls, website traffic and leads. Great reviews increase the click-thru rates on Google Adwords Express advertisements.

When speaking at a recent NADA Convention, a Honda dealer from New York asked me how his dealership could stand out in the final weeks of a consumer's car-purchasing decision. He prefaced the question by stating that in the crowded New York metro area there were multiple Honda dealers, just minutes away from his store.

He was convinced that he was normally one of the "finalists" in the decision-making process, but he wanted a bigger share of the purchases to be at his dealership. I challenged him with this question: "How do you know that your dealership wasn't eliminated from the list of considerations at the beginning of the consumer's research?" He had a puzzled expression. I clarified my position by asking, "What if your online reviews told this consumer you were a cheat, a fraud, you used bait-and-switch pricing tactics, or you have horrible service? Would they still want to buy from you?"

Pick any 10 dealers in a local market, read their Google Places reviews, and you will see why this challenge was appropriate. See what the last few reviews had to say about each dealership. For some dealers, the reviews are landmines that kill sales opportunities every day.

Dealers who take online reviews seriously and have a process in place to survey customers and encourage them to post online reviews will have an Unfair Advantage in their marketplace.

CHAPTER 20

Mobile Collides With Merchandising Strategies

By Jay Radke

This chapter will demonstrate how any dealership, whether it is a franchised operation or an independent used vehicle center, can unlock a secret weapon—one that is often overlooked.

Implementing an online vehicle merchandising strategy can produce numerous benefits that will help dealers achieve greater success in all areas of their online digital strategy, including enhanced communication with potential customers and a portrayal of transparency. Transparency today builds trust with online customers.

Proper online vehicle merchandising strategies also raises the level of product awareness and knowledge for the dealership's sales team. The concepts and strategies I will discuss may seem simple, but truth be told, they have been overlooked by dealers and vendors for the last decade.

My promise is that I will provide dealers with the foundation for a strategy that will unlock another Unfair Advantage, one that will help propel dealers past their competition.

Mickey Mantle was quoted saying, "It's unbelievable how much you don't know about the game you have been playing your entire life." The same can be said about the automotive industry in recent years.

AN INTRODUCTION TO MERCHANDISING

The 21st century consumer has been changed by the dominant influence of mobile technology. Consumers are now researching and connecting with products via the mobile web. This in itself can be a sizeable roadblock for traditional storefronts to adapt to. Capturing consumers at the right time in this modern-buying cycle relies on the execution of a great online merchandising strategy.

Merchandising by definition is the methods, practices and operations used to promote and sustain certain categories of commercial activity. In the broadest sense, merchandising is any practice that contributes to the sale of products to a retail consumer.

In 2012, online merchandising is the process that allows a retailer to go where the customers are. Over the last 10 years, the sales floor has moved from bricks and mortar to the internet and e-commerce websites.

As the 21st century continues to advance, the dynamics of all retail businesses will continue to be affected by the technology sector. The mobile device makers, search engines, social media sites and telecom companies will continue to push new boundaries by advancing society further and further ahead every day.

The mobile revolution has created a world where consumers and businesses enjoy great new services through the ever-present internet coverage supplied by advanced mobile networks that are deployed on multiple high-quality devices and create user experiences that allow for in-house processes that are far superior than any third-party contractor can deliver.

Mobile technology plays an active role in the lives of all business owners, customers, employees, and, of course, your day-to-day life. The opportunity and benefits of becoming a "mobile" dealer far outweigh holding on to the past.

The shift to mobile is what will take a dealer "live" and position them to truly compete in the online marketplace. Without the power of mobile technology, dealers will be unable to implement processes that enable their team to generate rich data on a real-time basis.

Technology platforms are now available like cDemo.com that enable dealers to configure their own data collection processes through smartphone apps. Dealers that adopt a mobile merchandising strategy initiated via a high-end smartphone will see dramatic improvements in their businesses, simply by replacing their old strategy that requires multiple devices. They almost immediately become faster, more organized and more effective merchandisers.

Overlooking the power of technology that is available today inhibits a dealer's ability to capitalize on the power of the mobile environment. Embracing mobile technology ultimately allows dealers to control profit-generating variables from the start of their online sales process.

Industry experts are predicting that in the near future we will be working and selling in a BYOD (Bring Your Own Device) work environment as devices and technology will continue to get faster and our old technology becomes more painful to use. *Go mobile or be left behind by your customers, staff and your competition.*

MERCHANDISING CAN BE YOUR SECRET WEAPON!

Properly merchandising cars is the first step in modern online automobile sales and drives the overall digital strategy of any dealership. The overlooked core competency in the automotive industry today is the commitment to a solid online merchandising strategy, a process that can be considered a secret weapon at this point in time.

Back in 2001, we had some inclination that technology was starting to explore and push the capabilities of mobile devices to new levels. Cameras and tablets started to be able to be synchronized together and data files could be pushed to websites via proprietary software solutions.

Fast forward to 2012, and you will see the global mobilization movement has picked up momentum in the last two years and will continue to gain traction. Mobile devices are tools that must have their own strategy. Participate or become extinct.

BUILDING FILTERS AROUND YOUR BUSINESS

Practices within the dealership environment in the past were structured to control the customer as they transitioned through the car buying lifecycle: *Disclose the minimum amount of information required in order to get the customer to the next step and then train, train, train the salespeople to overcome objections as they arise! Sound familiar?*

In today's online marketplace, if the dealership is not disclosing all the features, options, equipment, condition, photos and video about each and every vehicle in inventory up front, at the start of the purchasing lifecycle, then they are just creating a filter and giving online customers a reason to not contact you.

It is no longer the dealer's choice as to what type of information they provide for their inventory. Dealers today have to publish as much information as is required to enable the online customer to drill into the online transactional lifecycle.

Many customers are only going to facilitate research online and general product comparisons so a minimal amount of information would be adequate, but dealers are now selling up to 20 percnt of their used cars online, sight unseen, and the customers are just coming in for a pickup.

This is the point where the rubber meets the road. If there is any major discrepancy between what was published online and how the vehicle is actually equipped, dealers will have created either the best or worst customer at that point of delivery.

Online customers today are expecting that dealers know the exact details of what they are selling. If consumers spend hours or days researching online, collaborating, communicating, financing and even trading in their vehicle online and then they show up to find out the vehicle has a cloth interior instead of what was supposed to be leather...I think you can figure out the result.

THE VISION

In order to become a clear leader in your local market area, merchandising needs to be an anchoring process that will initiate the building of long-term relationships with retail customers and their referral networks.

THE PEOPLE

Any organization that wants to establish itself in the online transactional space requires high-quality people to take ownership of the merchandising strategy. Their efforts are critical to the success of capturing consumers at the earliest touch point in their shopping process. Ninety percent of consumer purchase decisions start online or are initiated from their mobile device. Having the dealer's best team in place to merchandise their products is the commitment they will need to make if they want to grow with the marketplace.

THE MEASUREMENTS

Over my 17-year career in the automotive industry, I have found one commonality in all the great dealership operators: They are all great at listening to the numbers. They all live and learn by what the numbers tell them. They measure and track everything by numbers.

A strong merchandising strategy is no different. The theory is sound, measurable and easy to track. A formula for success and the simplest way to measure this process is displayed in the graphic that follows. At cDemo, we call this your Inventory Health Score.

cDemo Merchandising Scorecard: The Measurements of Your Inventory Health

Each measurement in the scorecard is a critical factor in your inventory health success formula. The following details exactly what the scorecards tracks and how we use it to tell how well a dealer is doing.

- *Percentage of real photos:* Real photos create the instant feeling that the dealer actually has the car or truck in inventory. Stock photos, lack of photos, or the use of "photo coming soon" is another filter that suggests to an online customer that you either: a) do not have the car, or b) that you actually have no information on the vehicle you are displaying as available.

- *Quantity of photos:* Very simply put, 8 to 10 photos are not enough in today's online market—the more the better. A filter is placed on the dealership when it is perceived to be hiding missing faults, missing equipment, or being evasive by omitting detailed information.

- *Quality of content:* The rules of a dealer's showroom do not apply to the internet. It is not a game of cat and mouse online. In fact, it is quite the opposite. The more detailed dealers are with photos, video, options, equipment and disclosure of condition, the more likely the dealer will be able to move an online customer closer to a transaction. A filter is placed on a dealership when it chooses to play by the old rules and use the internet to fish rather than to sell. Remember, an online customer is only one click away from satisfying their need for information.

- *Percentage of live video:* In today's online sales environment, live video presentations is an overlooked strategy. Recently, YouTube videos have extremely high Search Engine Rankings.

To be clear, "live video" is not taking photos, putting them into a slideshow, and using a funky voice to explain the features of the car. Live video means taking the extra 3 minutes and 28 seconds to capture real video that can be found online to demonstrate the vehicle being offered for sale.

If live video is omitted from merchandising, dealers will place a filter around their store that leads an online customer to the conclusion that the dealership is taking a short-cut when it comes to demonstrating the vehicle with a photo slideshow and calling it live video. When done properly, video can allow your merchandising specialist to bring your store's personality to the online space. Live video can become a dealer's biggest lead generator.

- *Days to market:* This measurement may be one of the most important data points when it comes to the dealership's bottom line. Turning inventory faster and more often is now directly related to how quickly dealers get their inventory to the online marketplace.

Combining faster processes with the use of mobile data collection technology is a major profit-capturing benefit for any dealer. Very simple math can demonstrate how using one device and increasing your speed to market can produce great results.

Current model year cars and even cars that are two to three years old will drop in value by roughly $500 per month, or $18 per day, in the wholesale market. In extreme cases, you can see market fluctuations and value drops of $1,500 per month, or $50 per day.

In solid theory, the faster dealers get their cars to the online market, the more likely the dealer will hold on to the grosses they intended to make when they acquired the vehicle.

Most dealers carry 75 used cars and take an average of 12 days to get their cars online. By decreasing this time to one or two days to market, dealers potentially will capture an additional $13,500 in retained gross on the low end and $37,500 in the extreme markets.

Follow this math: 75 units x 10-day decrease x $18/day drop in value = $13,500. How is that for an unfair advantage?

THE BENEFITS

The ultimate goal in a dealership merchandising strategy should be to create more leads and sales, period. The most successful formula to create online transactions is driven by content that engages potential customers in such a way that they choose to transact with you.

That formula should be based on abundance, accuracy and credibility of the content you choose to share with them. Simply put—be transparent!

Sherwood Park Toyota: A Real World Example

Art Angielski, owner of Sherwood Park Toyota, says, "Advertising and merchandising are not the same, but when both are done right they work together to sell more cars. Properly merchandising our inventory is the driving force of our digital strategy."

Art briefly outlined their strategy:

1. The dealership has a dedicated in-house team that is responsible for merchandising all vehicles. They have to be physically fit, knowledgeable and detail oriented. Dedicated employees who take responsibility for the online inventory health of the dealership can dramatically affect the bottom line of a store. An underperforming salesperson is not the right choice.

2. Our merchandising strategy on every vehicle includes a minimum of over 35 actual photos, real video (not stitched photos with a funky voice-over), and full disclosure as it relates to condition and verifying all equipment and options. We also include our best price. The same can be said for wear-and-tear disclosures; the scratches and dings do not magically disappear when the customer arrives. I would rather be upfront with them online from the start.

3. Go mobile! Smartphones are no longer handicapped by quality or capabilities. They have become powerful tools of communication and connectivity. Having the ability to connect to back-end systems through a smartphone is a huge time-saving advantage. Vehicles can be merchandised and uploaded within minutes of arriving at our dealership when we use cDemo's Mobile Inspector app and dashboard. I no longer need to wait as we have taken control and now get our vehicles live online within hours versus days or even weeks.

---

cDemo's standardized data collection platform was founded on passion and a purpose. Our founders at cDemo built Mobile Inspector and the cDemo Platform to solve the challenges that merchandising purposefully solves. To summarize, the key points of this chapter:

- For dealerships that commit to a well-organized merchandising strategy, the benefits include more leads, more appointments set, higher close rates, and faster turns on their inventory. Dealers have no choice but to commit to a solid online merchandising strategy.

- All processes are measureable! The merchandising scorecard discussed above outlines exactly what to track and how well a dealer is doing.

- Merchandising solidifies a dealership's ability to motivate a consumer to want to make a purchase prior to dealing with a salesperson. The new online customer expects all the details and disclosures to be present. Remember, be transparent!

Exercise #1: Make contact with your dealership as an online customer. See if your staff can answer two or three questions about a car you are interested in, without saying "Can I get back to you"? If they have to get back to you later, you have a problem.

Exercise #2: For additional reading to compliment the theories in this chapter, order Dennis Galbraith's most recent book *Online Vehicle Merchandising*.

About Jay

Jay Radke is a Canadian entrepreneur who has been with cDemo. com since 2008 and currently holds the role of Vice President of Business Development for cDemo Mobile Solutions Ltd. cDemo Mobile Solutions is a recognized leader in Mobile App Data Collection Technology.

The cDemo team has developed and refined their product over a period of more than 10 years, resulting in a system that is very flexible and easily configured for any type of user or industry. Their cornerstone smartphone app, "Mobile Inspector, " is a very simple to use. Using only one device, the user is provided simple on-screen instructions detailing exactly what to do, requiring very little training or experience.

Prior to joining cDemo, Jay spent the majority of his career working in the wholesale side of the business in the auction, remarketing and fleet services industry with Enterprise Holdings Inc. as Group Remarketing and Acquisition Manager in Alberta, Canada, and St. Louis, Missouri. He oversaw a team responsible for the complete lifecycle of a fleet that peaked at over 50,000 automobiles throughout the year.

Gaining extensive industry knowledge from vehicle purchasing, ordering, marshalling, direct-to-dealer sales, auction resale initiatives and fleet planning for over 50,000 cars allows Jay to speak and share about a deep level of automotive industry knowledge. His passion lies in helping the automotive community move forward, and he has made the shift to apply his knowledge to the digital aspect of this great industry. His expertise comes from being a part of the development and launch of the cDemo Merchandising platform, which propelled his expertise in this area of the business.

CHAPTER 21

Social Media Marketing: Lightning in a Bottle

By Timothy Martell

Imagine a new car dealership in the late '90s. It's small, with a one-car showroom and eight sales professionals. The store is in a town of less than 30,000, on a two-lane road that is 12 miles from the nearest highway. The 15,000-square-foot dealership building is 40 years old and occupies 2.2 acres of land. The OEM planning volume for the store is 480 units, and it's located 30 miles from the nearest major city.

Fast forward to 2011, and that same store sold about 2,000 vehicles, generated $50 million in gross sales, and is the third-largest volume dealer in its region by new car sales volume (out of over 100 dealerships). As for used cars, the store is 22nd in the country for CPO sales volume. Yet with all that success, this dealership spent no money whatsoever on TV, radio or print in the last five years.

This dealership demonstrates that shifting traditional advertising investments to digital and social media strategies results in an effective, profitable business model. Dealers shouldn't be fearful about abandoning advertising strategies that worked in the past but no longer deliver a great ROI today.

While social media is not the sole reason for this dealer's success, it was the game changer for this store following 2008's economic collapse. Having firsthand knowledge of their strategy, I will share how dealers can achieve similar results using social media.

SOCIAL STRATEGIES FOR DEALERS

As we begin, it's important to dispel a few myths:

Myth #1: You can't sell with social media!

False: While it's true that social media is more like a "party" than a platform for sales, dealers can sell with social media. What they *can't* do is apply old techniques to this new medium. Shouting doesn't work in social media. Dealers need to draw consumers into their brand via common interests. In essence, social media can be viewed as a baiting technique.

Myth #2: It's not about numbers. It doesn't matter how many subscribers/likes/followers/+1s you have.

False: Let's be clear. It's *all* about numbers. Anyone asserting otherwise either doesn't have them or doesn't know how to get them.

Myth #3: Social media is only for kids or the college crowd.

False: Only 37 percent of Facebook's users and 53 percent of Twitter's are under 35. One of our clients just reached 25,631 followers on Facebook from their posts during the week. More than 36 percent of those followers were between 25 and 54 years old; 14.2 percent were over 55 years old. When's the last time your dealership was able to put their brand in front of 11,559 consumers... for free?

Did I just say free? I know; nothing is truly free. It takes either time or money to develop and deploy a strategy to acquire a consumer base to market to. However, those costs are fixed and not recurring. Therefore, every subsequent campaign forever reduces the cost per sale, meaning the ROI eventually becomes infinite.

See? Free!

THE PILLARS OF SOCIAL MEDIA

Social media, used correctly, is a powerful form of marketing. It is how loyalty is built and how a dealership insulates itself from brand abandonment. The beauty of social media is that a single customer's experience is amplified and felt by thousands of potential buyers as it ripples across their social networks.

For social media to work its magic, your dealership *must* have a presence in those social networks. The five pillars of social media are a blog, Facebook, Google +, Twitter and YouTube. Let's discuss each below.

Blog

The blog is a simple publishing tool to put a dealer's stories online without the need of a web programmer. The dealership blog essentially functions as the communication hub for all digital marketing assets. It can also power a dealer's in-house SEO efforts. On average, companies that blog get 55 percent more web traffic and 70 percent more leads than those that don't. Dealers thrive on leads, so they should embrace blogging.

Blogging Platforms

There has been a lot of controversy over the various blogging platforms and how they each use (or fail to use) SEO. I am going to put it to bed once and for all: Choose a blog that is based on WordPress.

Now to be clear, I am not talking about Wordpress.com. I am talking about building a blog on a unique domain or subdomain using the WordPress content management software (CMS). This is the strongest and simplest way a dealer can take control and produce tremendous results in terms of visual appeal and powerful SEO.

Find a reputable company to build a nicely designed blog on WordPress CMS technology. *Do not* fall for the free or included blog that comes with a dealer's website. For the sake of time, we will skip the technical jargon. Just know it has *serious* negative ramifications from an SEO standpoint. So make sure the blog is on its own domain or subdomain.

Content Writing

Once the dealership blog is built, it needs to be populated with quality content. There are a couple of ways dealers can approach content writing. If they have a capable writer internally, then he may be able to do this in-house. If not, then they can hire a service to handle the content production. Just be sure it's not getting dumped onto someone's plate. Remember, it needs to be quality content, every time.

While it's OK to blog about the company, dealer events and even sales promotions, it should also include consumer interest content that can veer well outside the automotive realm. A good rule of thumb is 2:1.

For every article written about some kind of sales promotion, two more should be written about something completely unrelated to sales and automotive.

Finally, the blog must be optimized using consistent SEO techniques. With that in place, a dealership should be well on its way to adding a component that will offer a significant competitive advantage by sending more traffic to the website, resulting in more leads.

Facebook

The simple truth is this: to be successful in marketing a car dealership on Facebook, one must accept the reality that *no one* is interested in being friends with a car dealership on Facebook. Facebook serves two basic functions: entertainment and social connectivity.

People do *not* go on Facebook to consciously research brands or products. People will talk about brands or products with people in their social network; they may even share an experience they've had with a company. But as a primary motivation, they don't seek out brands and products. However, brands and products *can* seek consumers, either by way of Facebook ads or by acquiring "likes" via a social marketing strategy.

What should be on a Facebook page? Cute, controversial, comical. Notice the word "sales" does not appear. A dealer posts a picture of a cute kitten: *good*. Another dealer posts a picture of a used car: *bad*.

Remember why people use Facebook. They want entertainment and something to talk about. Dealers must give local consumers something they want to share with their friends. When a fan of a dealer's Facebook page shares a picture, it lists the dealership's name right on the share window. Advanced dealers may even insert a small logo as a watermark on the picture.

If there is a major news story that the community is talking about, dealers should mention the "controversial" aspect of that story along with asking, "What do you think?" This strategy may spark discussion between a dealer's fans and other people in the community, which extends the dealership's brand awareness.

Facebook's new deals section allows businesses to offer incentives to consumers who check in on Facebook while at their location. This is a great way to entice the dealer's fans to help market their business for them. For example, "check in on Facebook when getting an oil change and get a free car-wash." When customers check in, they are sending an advertisement for the dealership to everyone they know! Speaking of incentives, dealers should not offer a prize in exchange for liking their Facebook page nor can they offer a chance to win for liking a page. It's a violation of Facebook's TOS and ultimately just a bad marketing decision.

Google+ for Dealers

Google has the largest user base of any online entity. Daily, billions of searches are conducted on Google. Google, being well aware of that fact, has strategically integrated the "Google Plus Project" into their search platform. When Google account-holders search for anything, they receive customized search results that include social "likes" from people they're connected to. Often, if the dealer's website does not rank for a search term, but a friend of the searcher rated it highly, the website could be moved to page one.

In many respects the Google+ social network is peripheral from the standpoint of a local car dealer. It can be easy to dismiss it as "bleeding edge." While I wouldn't advocate focusing a huge financial investment to develop a presence on Google+, it's undeniably necessary, and dealers need to publish quality content regularly.

The SEO ramifications from Google+ alone dictate that this platform cannot be ignored. Past experiences with Google suggest that getting there first brings long-lasting rewards.

Twitter

Twitter is a social networking service that lets users share 140 character posts. Why it may be useful to a business or a brand, it can be nebulous, so instead of trying to define it, let's focus on some facts.

There will be nearly 21 million Twitter users in the U.S. by 2013. A sizable minority of those will use the service, at least in part, to follow brands.

34 percent of marketers have generated leads using Twitter, and 20 percent have closed deals using Twitter.

There are now 100 million active users; 50 million log in at least once a month or more, and 50 million users log in at least once a day!

40 percent don't tweet anything! They just check their timeline to keep tabs on what people are saying.

The sheer volume of users makes Twitter compelling. The bottom line is, even if all dealers are going to do is "shout," they will have a significant advantage over dealers that aren't there.

A note about frequency: Tweet often, tweet well. The average lifespan of a tweet is three minutes. This makes it virtually impossible to offend a following by oversharing, as Twitter is really just a noisy room where everyone is talking. Twitter's advanced search function allows the user to "turn down" the noisy room and dial into very specific conversations. In addition to being keyword specific, the user can select conversations that take place within a certain radius of a particular location.

With this information, a dealer could spend a few short minutes every morning looking for people mentioning their vehicles within X miles of their dealership and create opportunities.

Nearly once a week I am able to find a post on Twitter within 50 miles of a dealer I may be working with who has tweeted something to the effect of "Yup, the [insert vehicle here] died on me yesterday. Looks like it's time for a new car." Or "Yikes! [insert vehicle] just crapped out! Anyone know a good tow service?"

Now imagine what a dealer could do to impress a potential consumer armed with this sort of information!

YouTube
YouTube is unique in that it's a search engine, traditional SEO tool, *and* a social media tool. Many dealers overlook using YouTube as part of their digital strategy.

Dealers must commit to creating videos in-house to use in conjunction with their social platforms. Dealers are never limited on what they can shoot on video; be creative. Celebrate your dealership by recording things like customer testimonials, employee achievements, and amenities at the dealership. Additionally, dealers should record video tutorials to assist customers on things like programming remotes/Bluetooth/memory-seats/navigation or the vehicle address book.

The key to a strong video marketing strategy is to vary the content. Information is great and dealers should want to be a resource for knowledge, but people share things about people. The more "human" the dealer becomes, the more humans will come to the dealer.

SOCIAL MEDIA BY THE NUMBERS

Still not convinced? Here are more social media statistics:

- 33 percent of social media users surveyed said that they would prioritize social media freedom, device flexibility, and work mobility over salary in accepting a job offer.

- 43 percent of all online consumers are social media fans or followers.

- 64 percent of Americans stream mobile video at work.

- 245 million internet users exist in the U.S., according to Internet World, while Nielsen estimates that social media sites and blogs reach 80 percent of all active U.S. internet users!

- Social media and blogs account for 43 percent of all internet usage, according to another Nielsen study.

In other words, if you want to be taken seriously by consumers in digital marketing, you better take social media seriously.

PUT IT ALL TOGETHER

By now you might be thinking, "How can a dealer use a blog, a Facebook page, a Google+ page, a Twitter page and YouTube to get anyone to come to the dealership?"

Here's the forest through the trees...

It's 8 am Monday morning, and that scheduled blog post just went live containing the YouTube video of Nissan's new social media-driven project car. The 2,962 people who read the dealer's blog every month just found out.

But wait, the article also posted to their 91,133 fans on Facebook, the 97,035 followers on Twitter, and the 2,801 people who have the dealership in their circles on Google +. It's 8:01 am, and 193,931 people just had a chance to see ABC Nissan's name and a story about their brand.

Within an hour, 182 people liked it on Facebook, 97 people commented, and 35 people shared it with another 4,550 of their friends. Seventy-four people have retweeted the link to the article, sending 360 new readers to the blog. Twenty-six of them decide to subscribe to it, 152 people Stumbled the article, seven people Dugg it, and six people Tumbl'd it.

The above scenario was an actual account of one of my dealer clients. It's important to note that this is not a stand-out performance but rather an average morning post that happens three times a day, seven days a week. While results like these take time to achieve, they are in no way atypical.

Results like these can be achieved every day all month long for less than the cost of a weekend ad in a major newspaper or a handful of cable TV spots. In fact, the cost of the average direct mail campaign would pay for 10 months of this type of service.

You are now armed with information that *most* of your competition will fail to use. Use it now—and get an unfair advantage over your competition today!

To stay up to date on the latest social media information as well as bonus material made to accompany this book, please visit www. unfairadvantage.co.

About Timothy

Timothy Martell is a marketing expert regularly sought out by both media and industry leaders for his opinion on social media marketing campaigns that really work. Timothy has been seen on "MSNBC" and "Dateline"; interviewed twice by Facebook for his successful dealership advertising campaigns; a featured speaker at automotive conferences, such as DMSC, AMBC, and the Driving Sales Executive Summit; and featured on the cover of *AutoSuccess* magazine. Timothy is known for pushing the boundaries of conventional automotive thinking and producing social media campaigns that generate massive numbers of followers leading to record ROI. Timothy founded Wikimotive in 2010, a company that provides all encompassing digital marketing strategies for automotive dealerships including website design, mobile website design, customized SEO, and social media marketing that focuses on targeting and acquiring many thousands of consumers who ultimately become followers of his client's social media outlets.

Critically acclaimed as a "Social Media Rockstar," Timothy's marketing systems consistently produce results that are of "Rockstar" status. Wikimotive's social media management systems remove the tedium of finding and identifying consumer-engaging content from the dealer all while educating the dealer's key personnel on how to use the most important social media platforms in order to generate and retain business.

To learn more about Timothy Martell and Wikimotive, and to find out how to receive a free digital marketing evaluation, visit www.wikimotive.com or call (508) 561-1945.
www.wikimotive.com
facebook.com/Wikimotive
twitter.com/wikimotive

Solving the Puzzle

By Tracy Myers

In the introduction to this book, I talked about how running an auto dealership is a bit like doing a jigsaw puzzle. I went on to say that it's actually a lot more complicated than that as the big benefit of dong a jigsaw puzzle is that you start out with all the right pieces and with a picture on the front of the box.

In this book, Brian and I aimed to help you identify the most important pieces you need to have in place in order to solve the puzzle of building a successful and profitable auto dealership in today's highly competitive marketplace.

The experts in the team we assembled have shared some powerful insights into the most important elements of staying ahead of the competition and creating success. We identified all the most important pieces you need to have in place through:

- Foundations
- Technology
- Process
- Operations
- Marketing

We started by addressing the importance of building your successful dealership on strong foundations. We looked at how to position yourself as an expert so your dealership becomes the obvious first choice in your market.

We also outlined the steps you need to take to engage your target audience with that message through a combination of traditional, digital and social media techniques. Important as these steps are, none of us has unlimited time so we showed you how to make it as easy as possible to put this in place.

Then we went on to cover technology. This is one of the most challenging pieces of the puzzle for many dealers, yet it presents some of the greatest opportunities for those who are ready to harness it.

That's why we brought together top experts in some of the most important areas of technology. We showed you how to create the best possible dealer websites and looked at how adding extra services such as chat can add considerable value.

OPPORTUNITIES FOR GROWTH

These days, one of the most significant growth areas in business is the use of mobile, whether in smartphone apps, SMS marketing or mobile advertising. This offers huge advantages for those dealers who are ready to harness it—and a huge threat for those who don't have access to the right resources and information.

In this book, we have given you access to some of the latest insights in these fields, giving you a chance to get a few steps ahead of your competitors.

Mobile marketing is one field that is continuing to develop very rapidly. This allows you to take full advantage of one of the powerful benefits we included in this book: regular updating of the information to reflect development and progress.

BEYOND TECHNOLOGY

Despite all the growing capabilities of technology, it's never been more crucial to have the right processes for connecting with customers and prospects. In an increasingly competitive world, the quality of our sales skills is more important than ever and gives us a chance to stand out. That's why we devoted a section of the book to this topic.

And while new technology expands quickly, that "old" technology of the telephone remains one of the most important of all. Getting these traditional approaches right can make the difference between becoming one of those who succeed instead of one of those who do not.

Of course, the overall success of your dealership depends on the quality of your operations. It can be easy to let these everyday issues fade into second place as they may not seem as exciting as the latest developments in technology or social media.

Getting your merchandising right remains a crucial piece of the puzzle and not being on top of pricing can just mean you keep failing to make the sale. If you follow the advice we included here, you will not make those mistakes. We also talked about other important aspects of your operations such as reinsurance.

Getting all these parts of the business right allows you to take advantage of the success you have in the other areas we talked about.

STRATEGY FOR SUCCESS

One of the most vital pieces of the puzzle is getting the marketing right. So it's perhaps not surprising we devoted a great deal of the book to this element.

While we spent a lot of time talking about the tactics you use and how to get the best from them, we highlighted the importance of having a strong strategy in place that flows all the way through from your initial marketing to the final steps in the sales process.

We emphasized the steps you need to take to make this unique to your dealership so people have a reason to choose you over others.

While we spent a lot of time talking about technology and cutting-edge developments, such as social media, we took time to highlight the importance of more conventional approaches, such as direct mail.

Many businesses are putting so much time and effort into trying to understand the newer areas of marketing that they miss out on the opportunities to use these approaches. This creates massive opportunities for those wise business owners who still pay attention to the proven marketing approaches. That's why we included them here.

With so much business now coming through online contact points, we paid a lot of attention to how to get more visitors to your website using search engine optimization and search engine marketing.

It is so easy to either miss out on these opportunities or to end up paying through the nose instead of benefiting from free traffic or getting the best value possible from paid-for advertising. We wanted to help you get maximum bang from your bucks and to make sure you are not wasting money and opportunity in those areas.

THE POWER OF VIDEO

One of the most exciting areas of marketing these days is the use of video. This can seem intimidating to people without the right information. We wanted to share how easy it is to use video to start attracting large numbers of prospects and customers to your dealership. I encourage you not to wait and allow your competitors to beat you to that benefit.

We also sought to provide a relevant guide through the intricacies of social media. Getting this right can open up huge new opportunities for your business but can be a big waste for people who don't have access to the type of information included here.

Without having access to the right information, many people are scared off because they see it as too challenging to get involved in these areas. Others have been put off because they have tried it without the right guidance and have wasted time and money doing the wrong things.

This book is about making sure you have access to the knowledge and strategies you need to make the most of the potential of all of the areas we discussed.

The case studies we included are designed to show you a practical way to start implementing these ideas in your dealership. I encourage you to review them several times and consider how you can apply the lessons in your dealership.

TAKING ACTION

Of course, all this information is useless if you don't put it into practice, and that's why we paid a lot of attention to helping you develop an action plan so you start seeing results quickly.

Our aim in this book has been to give you the information you need so you can start to solve the puzzle of how to create greater success in your dealership. I hope we have helped you develop a clear picture of the success you can achieve. I hope we have also helped you identify the most important strategies you need to put in place and how to implement them best.

Our aim is that you should feel you have a team of experts on hand that you can turn to when you want to move your business further forward. You should also be better placed to decide which strategies are most important and how best to start implementing them.

One of the things that make this book different is that it doesn't stop with the guidance of a team of top experts. Their advice is constantly updated, so you can be sure you are not getting dated information, but rather access to cutting-edge insights.

Not only that, the community you are part of goes beyond you and the authors. It extends to a wide group of other passionate industry experts who are willing to share their insights and help you move your dealership forward.

I am delighted to have you as part of that community and look forward to hearing details of your success.

—*Tracy Myers*